45p

D0434307

Puffin Books
Editor: Kaye Webb

THE DODO, THE AUK AND THE ORYX

'As dead as a dodo' is a sadly common expression. Sad because no one in living memory has ever seen a dodo, and the world is a sadder place for it.

Some kinds of animals have died out naturally, because they were no longer adapted to live in the world as it changed, but man with his superior weapons and intelligence is the most dangerous threat to the animal world there has ever been. The dodo was large and harmless: it died because it couldn't survive the settlement of its home, Mauritius, by men and their domesticated animals. How many other creatures have we driven, or are we driving, to extinction?

In the fifty years between 1851 and 1901 thirty-one kinds of mammal disappeared, and today about six hundred forms of animal life are near vanishing point. Robert Silverberg tells the story of some birds and beasts which have vanished from the earth and others which have been rescued from extinction. Today we are making some effort to preserve our wild life: it is worth preserving. Just imagine how dull the world would be without tigers, elephants, hummingbirds, aardvarks and kangaroos!

Cover design by Patrick Oxenham

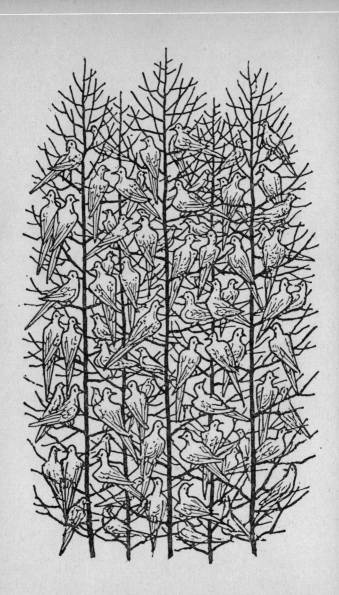

Robert Silverberg

The Dodo, the Auk and the Oryx

Vanished and Vanishing Creatures

Illustrated by Jacques Hnizdovsky

Puffin Books

Puffin Books: a Division of Penguin Books Ltd,
Harmondsworth, Middlesex, England
Penguin Books Australia Ltd, Ringwood,
Victoria, Australia

First published in the U.S.A. as
The Auk, The Dodo and the Oryx, 1967
Published in Great Britain by World's Work 1969
Published in Puffin Books 1973
Reprinted 1974
Copyright © Robert Silverberg, 1967

Made and printed in Great Britain by
Cox & Wyman Ltd, London, Reading and Fakenham
Set in Linotype Georgian

Contents

When I hear of the destruction of a species I
feel as if all the works of some great writer had
perished.

THEODORE ROOSEVELT, 1899

It is the responsibility of all who are alive today
to accept the trusteeship of wildlife
and to hand on to posterity,
as a course of wonder and interest,
knowledge and enjoyment,
the entire wealth of diverse animals and plants.
This generation has no right
by selfishness
wanton or unintentional destruction,
or neglect,
to rob future generations of this great heritage.
Extermination of other creatures
is a disgrace to mankind.

THE WORLD WILDLIFE CHARTER, 1962

Passenger Pigeon

I

The Idea of
Extinction

The whitened bones of strange creatures line the galleries of our museums. Here, all fangs and claws, is the nightmarish figure of a great dinosaur. There stands the eerie skeleton of an ancient amphibian who carried on his back a huge bony sail. Along this wall are mounted the remains of a mighty serpent of the sea.

These are the vanished ones, the extinct ones. They seem to us like creatures from another world. Indeed, that is what they are – creatures from a world mankind never knew, a world unthinkably remote in time. When these ancient beasts lived, the human race was still unborn. Fifty million years or more have passed since the monstrous dinosaurs stalked the earth. No man ever glimpsed them when they lived.

We know these animals of an earlier day only by the relics they have left us. Bones preserved in mud, the imprint of a scaly hide against the sand of a prehistoric beach, an outline cast in volcanic ash – these are the clues that tell us of the life of the past. The evidence of fossil bones helps us to know what sort of inhabitants the world had long ago. (The word *fossil* comes from the Latin word *fossilis*, which means 'dug up'.) Scientists uncovering fossils in the earth have been able to construct a picture of the extinct animals that once occupied our globe.

The beasts of a hundred million years ago seem incredibly alien to us. It is hard for us to see them as living creatures; we meet them as bones in a museum, and putting flesh on those bones is a difficult act of the imagination. But that is not to say that all extinct forms of life date from unthinkably ancient epochs. The museums have many exhibits that tell sorrowful tales of recent extinctions.

Here is a stuffed bird the size of a pigeon, nesting on a dozen buff-and-green eggs. No one will ever see this bird alive again. It is the heath hen, which was common in the north-eastern United States when George Washington was President. The last heath hen died in 1932. A curtain has fallen on that species, cutting it off for ever from our view.

Here is the skeleton of another bird, much larger, much stranger. It looks terribly clumsy, with its bulky body and awkward little legs and its huge, hook-billed head. It is the dodo, a native of a remote group of islands in the Indian Ocean. The last time anyone saw a live dodo was about three hundred years ago.

This giant skeleton, more than ten feet high, belongs to a moa – a bird of New Zealand that must have been truly awesome to behold. We can never view a live moa in all its majesty. Perhaps the moa still existed a few hundred years ago, but now it is gone for all time.

One more curious bird stares sightlessly out from its museum case: the great auk. It looks a little like a penguin, with its flipper-like feet and its upright stance, but its odd beak, large and unusual, marks it as something else. Hunters roaming the islands of the North Atlantic several centuries ago found great auks by the millions, and captured them to feed the settlers of the New World. It seemed impossible that there would ever be a time when none were left; but today the great auk is extinct.

There are many other names on the roster of recently extinct creatures. The quagga, the passenger pigeon, Steller's sea cow, the spectacled cormorant, the giant ground sloth – they are all just names now. They will never again be seen alive.

The process of extinction continues all the time. In fact, it is speeding up. Since the time of Christ, more than one hundred major species of mammals, two hundred species of birds, and a great many fish and reptiles have become extinct. Most of these have vanished within very recent times, as mankind's numbers have expanded and the animals have been driven from their homes.

Between 1801 and 1850, only two known kinds of mammals became extinct: the eastern bison of North America, and the Hispaniola hutia, a small rodent of the West Indies. But from 1851 to 1900, as hunters armed with modern weapons went to work, thirty-one kinds of mammals and many beautiful birds were wiped out. It was during this period that the passenger pigeon and the quagga were taken from the world.

Forty more forms of mammal life perished between 1901 and 1944. Some were obscure creatures whose passing went unnoticed except by scientists. Some were important local varieties, such as the Barbary lion of Africa, the Japanese wolf, and the Texas grizzly bear. And the extinctions continue. Today about six hundred mammal forms, and hundreds of bird and reptile species, are near the vanishing point. Only a handful exist of the superb Arabian antelope known as the oryx. There are about two dozen Javan rhinoceroses left. Less than fifty whooping cranes remain. A thousand blue whales survive. All over the world, tiny remnants of such dwindling species cling to life – while the thinning of the ranks goes on. It is possible that our grandchildren will never see many of the rare animals that still exist today.

Mankind has robbed the world of many irreplaceable forms of life, and it has much to answer for. We have been poor custodians of the creatures with whom we should have shared our world. Only in the last sixty years has there been any large-scale effort to save the vanishing species before it is too late.

Extinctions occurred before mankind appeared, though. We have hastened the disappearance of many forms of life, but not all the blame lies at our door. The dinosaurs became extinct without our help. Fossil evidence shows that thousands of species came and went before we existed. It seems that there is a natural course of development for any living race – a time of youth for a species, followed by a time of maturity, and then the death of the species. From moment to moment the world changes. All is in constant flux, and species pass as well as individuals.

This was recognized about two thousand years ago by the Roman poet Lucretius. He composed a lengthy poem, *On the Nature of Things*, in which he summed up most of the scientific knowledge of his time. Lucretius wrote:

'Nothing remains for ever what it was. Everything is on the move. Everything is transformed by nature and forced into new paths. One thing, withered by time, decays and dwindles. Another emerges from ignominy, and waxes strong. So the nature of the world as a whole is altered by age.'

Lucretius had many fanciful and improbable ideas about the universe, but his insight into the process of extinction was clear and shrewd. 'Many species must have died out altogether and failed to reproduce their kind,' he declared. 'Every species that you now see drawing the breath of life has been protected and preserved from the beginning of the world either by cunning or by prowess or by speed. In addition, there are many that survive under human protection because their usefulness has commended them to our care. The surly breed of lions, for instance, in their native ferocity have been preserved by prowess, the fox by cunning, and the stag by flight.'

He foreshadowed one of the main ideas of Charles Darwin's theory of evolution by calling attention to the competitive nature of the world. Those animals clever enough or strong enough or fast enough to overcome adversity would survive; others would fall by the wayside and die out. Some, because they were valuable to mankind, would get special protection and so would be exempt from the harsh laws of universal competition in nature. Lucretius never saw the fossil skeleton of a dinosaur, but he would not have been at all surprised to learn of such a creature. The idea of extinction was quite logical to him.

The coming of Christianity made that idea a forbidden one. For more than a thousand years, the teachings of the Bible were regarded as the literal truth. The Bible declared that God had created the heaven and the earth and all its creatures within the space of six days. The birds and beasts and fish were brought forth at one time. There was nothing in the Bible that said some animals might appear at later times. Nor was anything said about the possibility that certain types of animals might disappear. Everything created at once, and all species unchangeable and immortal – so the Scriptures maintained.

This view was enforced throughout medieval times, when the Christian Church was so strong that it could persecute anyone who disagreed with its beliefs. Probably some men privately held their own ideas about the nature of life, but they did not dare to speak out. Even after the various Protestant groups began to split away from the original church in the sixteenth century, the old teachings were maintained.

Thus Martin Luther, the first great leader of the Protestant movement, insisted on full acceptance of the words of Scripture. 'I hold that the animals took their being at once upon the word of God, as did also the fishes in the sea,' he said. A century later, in 1650, Archbishop James Ussher of the Irish city of Armagh calculated from the ages of people mentioned in the Bible and concluded that the world had been created in 4004 B.C. That did not leave much time for the coming and going of living creatures.

However, miners digging in the earth frequently came upon the bones of long-dead animals. Workers excavating for the foundations of new houses and churches also made such discoveries. A close look at these fossil bones showed that they were not the remains of any known creatures. Some were of great size; others were oddly different in shape from anything that had ever been studied. What were these fossils? Could it be that they were the relics of extinct animals?

That violated the accepted religious teachings. The churches still insisted that God had created all creatures at once, and that whatever God had created would survive unchanged until the Day of Judgment.

So many ingenious explanations were offered to account for the fossil finds. In the eleventh century one philosopher suggested that they were stones that simply happened to take the form of bones. In the thirteenth century, the notion was advanced that the fossils were 'models of God's rejected works' or 'outlines of future creations'. But these flimsy ideas were hard to support. The learned men went back to the Bible and found the phrase, 'There were giants in the earth in those days.' The big bones, obviously, were the remains of those early giants!

A good deal was known about anatomy by this time, though, and it was apparent that some of the bones belonged to weird and unfamiliar animals and could not possibly be the relics of giant human beings. A new explanation was produced that at last allowed the idea of extinction to gain a foothold.

Some animals, it was agreed by the church leaders, actually had become extinct. These were the ones that had not been taken into Noah's ark. When the deluge came, these creatures were allowed by God to perish. All the strange fossils that had been discovered were the bones of such *antediluvian*, or pre-deluge, animals.

This in itself was a compromise with the strict Biblical teaching, for the Bible said that God had ordered Noah to bring into the ark 'every living thing of all flesh'. But a compromise was needed to explain away the fossils. The progress of science brought new strains to the theory soon enough, for hundreds of species of animals were discovered by European explorers in such far-away places as America and Australia. Had all these been in the ark, too? If they had, how was it that the kangaroos had landed only in Australia when Noah let the animals ashore after the flood?

These troublesome questions punctured the deluge theory in many places. The world was full of different kinds of creatures, too numerous to explain away in terms of a single moment of creation, and all sorts of fossils had been unearthed, too numerous to explain away in terms of a single destroying deluge. Nor was it still easy to believe that the world had been created in 4004 B.C. The mounting scientific evidence indicated, by the late eighteenth century, that the world was much older than that, and had contained a great many types of life that no longer existed.

Baron Georges Cuvier, a leading French naturalist of that time, drew a chart showing all the epochs of past life. Cuvier believed that there had been several deluges and catastrophes, each one wiping out most of the creatures that lived. After each catastrophe, said Cuvier, God had created new forms of life. One of Cuvier's followers calculated that there had been no less than twenty-seven such world-wide catastrophes and new creations.

This elaborate theory was the last serious attempt to reconcile the Biblical ideas with the findings in the earth. In the nineteenth century it became clear that the world was millions or even billions of years old. A continuous process of creation went on all the time, so it was not necessary to invoke a series of catastrophes to explain the fossil record. Charles Darwin and others put forth the concept of *evolution* – the change in the forms of living things as they responded to the pressure of their environment and other forces.

Darwin showed that a process of natural selection weeds out the unfit creatures and encourages the multiplication of those that are most capable of surviving. Often climate and environment in a given place change radically. Those animals flexible enough to adapt to such changes in their environment endure; those that cannot adapt die out. Darwin saw the life of each species as an unending series of challenges and responses. Challenge brought change. If a challenge were too great for a species to meet, it would bring extinction.

Darwin bolstered his theory with the evidence gathered by science. He used fossils to illustrate the course of past evolution, showing how the forms of living animals had been quite different in the past. Not all creatures evolved at the same speed, Darwin said. Some, like the horshoe crab and the dragonfly and the cockroach, had not changed in any significant way in many millions of years. Darwin called these creatures 'living fossils'. They seemed to be immune to evolution; actually, they were so tough or so adaptable that there was no need for them to evolve to meet changing conditions, and they remained as they were.

Other animals and plants evolved much more swiftly – including man himself. This was the most controversial part of Darwin's theory. The evolutionists included mankind among the animals and said that we had developed from earlier forms. This produced an uproar that did not die away even when the fossils of odd-looking prehistoric types of men were discovered. Today some religious groups still firmly oppose the theory of evolution because it contradicts the Biblical story of creation.

The attempts to deny the theory have become increasingly more desperate as the scientific evidence has mounted. One of the last scientists to try to fight the wave of new ideas was the English naturalist Philip Gosse. In 1857, after a lifetime of careful observation of living things, Gosse published a book that backed the old theory of creation in 4004 B.C. He said that all the supposed signs of a greater antiquity – fossils, geological patterns, the scratches of ancient glaciers on rocks, and so forth – were merely 'appearances', proving nothing. God had created the world all at once, said Gosse, and He had chosen for reasons of His own to create these 'appearances' of a former existence. Gosse was able to conclude that 'the field is left clear and undisputed for the one witness . . . whose testimony is as follows: "In six days Jehovah made heaven and earth, the sea, and all that in them is." '

Few scientists would share this view today. The Biblical story of creation is accepted as a symbolic tale, not as literal truth. Modern scientists believe that the earth is some 3 to 5 thousand million years old. The first living things are thought to have emerged about 2 thousand million years ago. They were simple, one-celled plants and animals. Through a long, incredibly slow process of evolution, more complicated organisms appeared: worms and sponges and corals, fish, amphibians, reptiles, and then, rather late in the sequence of development, the warm-blooded animals known as mammals. Along this route of evolution many species were found wanting and died out, leaving only fossil traces behind. About two-thirds of all the animal species that ever existed are extinct today.

Until the advent of man, with his formidable skill for destruction, it was a slow business for species to die out. We have killed entire species of abundant creatures in a matter of fifty years or less, but in the past it sometimes required thousands or even millions of years for extinction to overtake a race. For this reason scientists draw the distinction between extermination and extinction. Most – though not all – of the recently extinct animals were exterminated by enemies. Extermination is swift, extinction slow. We can understand extermination easily, but natural extinction is still a scientific mystery.

One of the puzzles of extinction is the way it engulfed

whole populations of animals simultaneously at several times in the past. For instance, the dominant creature of the world one and a half thousand million years ago was a sea-dwelling crab-like animal known as a trilobite. There were many different sorts of trilobites, differing widely in size and appearance. For hundreds of millions of years they were the most common animals on earth.

Then they began to disappear. Abruptly, all but a few species of trilobites became extinct. The surviving types lasted for another 200 million years, but then they died out, too. The mass extinction of the trilobites took place about 500 million years ago. It appears that within a span of a million years or so, the majority of the trilobites vanished. That may not seem particularly abrupt, but a million years is actually only a moment, in comparison with the hundreds of millions of years during which they ruled the earth.

What made the trilobites perish so suddenly?

We do not know. Their time was up, and they disappeared – but that does not explain what happened. Nor can we blame their downfall on the rise of the first fishes, some 350 million years ago. The trilobites were already on the way out when the fishes appeared. No doubt this new breed of fast, agile sea creatures made life difficult for the trilobites, competing with them for food and even eating their eggs. Yet fishes and trilobites lived side by side for millions of years, striking some kind of balance. The last trilobites developed grotesque spiny protuberances and other strange features that served no apparent function. This is often a sign that a race is nearing extinction – in its old age it frequently evolves curious enlargements and excrescences. When the trilobites finally disappeared, it was not because the fishes had exterminated them; it was because they had somehow exhausted their racial vitality, and had reached a point where they could no longer sustain themselves. Each year more trilobites died than were born, until in the end no new ones at all were born.

Much the same thing happened about 250 million years ago when another widespread wave of extinction carried off nearly half of the animal types that then existed. Perhaps some general change in the world's climate fostered this mass extinction. Among the victims were the last trilobites, and also many races that had risen more recently to prominence. More than 75 per cent of the existing amphibian families and 80 per cent of the reptile families died out. So did various shellfish and crustaceans.

The way was cleared for a new group of dominant creatures. The age of dinosaurs opened. Those reptiles that had survived the last general extinction now flourished and grew huge. For 150 million years the giant reptiles occupied the earth almost to the exclusion of other forms of life. Though many types of dinosaurs became extinct within this period, the group as a whole remained dominant. Then, about 70 million years ago, the time came for their disappearance. Some types of reptiles survived – snakes and crocodiles, turtles, and lizards – but nearly all of the huge species died out. Once again the time of extinction was unusually swift in relation to the time that the species had spent on earth.

The next lords of the planet were the mammals. Here, again, one species succeeded another in great rapidity. Few of today's mammals look much like their ancestors of 20 or 30 million years ago. The horse, then, was hardly bigger than a dog; the rhinoceros, on the other hand, was far larger than the largest of modern elephants. These early types of mammals passed away, some dying out entirely, others evolving into the present-day forms. The evolutionary process operated with wonderful fertility, yielding species after species and discarding the ones that could not take firm hold.

This pattern of evolution and extinction is something we know about without really being able to explain. The fossil record tells us that whole species, just like individuals, go through stages of youth, maturity, and old age, followed by death. The cycle may be relatively swift, passing from evolution to extinction in a million years or less; or it may be incredibly slow, taking hundreds of millions of years. But evidently it happens to all creatures. No matter how vigorous a species is, no matter how numerous, it eventually comes to the downhill side of its curve of development, and slopes towards extinction. Perhaps its natural environment changes, making survival of the individual more hazardous. The weather is not as favourable; new enemies lurk nearby. Over thousands of generations, deaths begin to exceed births, until a point is reached when the species is doomed. When only a few thousand individuals remain, the probability of immediate extinction becomes overwhelmingly large.

To this natural factor of extinction was added a new element about a million years ago. It was then – just a moment ago, really, on the scale of evolutionary time – that the upright mammal known as man made his debut.

Since man walked on his hind legs, he had his hands free for the use of weapons. Since man had a brain better than that of any other creature, he soon learned how to employ weapons against the animals around him. He discovered the techniques of making use of the world. He lacked suitable claws and teeth for killing and cutting, so he invented axes and spears and knives. He found many uses for the animals about him: their flesh was his food, their hides clothed him, their bones became the points of his weapons and tools. His power to kill outstripped the ability of many animals to make good through reproduction the losses in their numbers. And so, as man gradually extended his empire, the normal process of extinction was coupled with a new process of extermination. For many animals, the odds against survival became too high. In Europe, Asia and Africa the toll of extinction began to mount.

One place where nature did not feel the impact of man was the New World. Apparently there were no humans in the Americas until thirty to forty thousand years ago, when roving bands of hunters crossed out of Asia via the Bering Strait, entering Alaska and filtering downwards into both continents. Until then, the archaic types of animals long since exterminated in Europe continued to exist here.

Elephants and camels and rhinoceroses still roamed the Americas. Woolly bison and huge wolves were found, and the fierce-looking sabre-toothed tiger, and giant bears, beavers, and elks. It was a hunter's paradise. When mankind finally entered these untouched continents, the killing began. About the same time there was a radical change in climate; the Americas grew much warmer, making life difficult for the big shaggy beasts of a cooler time.

The combination of climatic change and human hunting proved too much. About ten thousand years ago most of the big mammals of the New World became extinct. The charred bones of mammoths and tigers have been found at the camp sites of these ancient hunters, so we know that early man preyed on them for food. However, there were not many men in the New World during the time of this great extinction. The widely scattered bands of hunters may never have numbered more than a hundred thousand at any one time. So it is probably not correct to say that the hunters exterminated the big animals of the Americas. Rather, they sped the process of extinction, cutting down herds that already were being thinned by the changes in climate.

Once man learned how to domesticate animals and raise crops, the threat to wildlife multiplied many times over. The human population had always remained small so long as man had to depend on hunting and on gathering wild fruits for food. Now, nourished by the yield of his farms and livestock, man could expand. The population of the world increased vastly after the first settled agricultural communities appeared, some ten thousand years ago, and the rate of increase has grown bigger all the time. The most dramatic gains in human numbers have come in the last few hundred years.

There is no doubt now why animals are continuing to become extinct. The natural process of extinction still operates, but man the exterminator destroys in a few decades species that might otherwise have survived for thousands or millions of years. In the present century an average of one species a year is wiped out by man. Many of these extinctions were the result of the greed of our great-grandfathers, who brought hundreds of animals to such low population levels that the life of the species was endangered.

The Dodo, the Auk and the Oryx

Some animals have been slaughtered indiscriminately for food: the passenger pigeon, for instance, which was so tasty that it was hunted until none remained. Some extinctions are the result of man's vanity; in the last century many lovely birds were killed because women wanted to use their plumage to decorate hats and dresses and today the leopard, whose elegant hide is desired for purses and coats, is nearing the same fate.

Often we have deliberately sought to drive a species into extinction – as in the nineteenth century, when we all but wiped out the American bison so that the Indians who depended on it for food would suffer. We have also destroyed species in a kind of mindless ignorance, without even realizing what we were doing. Late in the nineteenth century, for example, fortifications were built on Great Gull Island, at the entrance of Long Island Sound, New York. In the course of this work many tons of soil were shifted about; and when the job was done, it was found that the workmen had accidentally buried the nesting places of a small creature known as the Gull Island meadow mouse, which existed nowhere else in the world. In that way mankind unintentionally doomed an inconspicuous rodent. By the time the accident was discovered, the last bells had tolled for the Gull Island meadow mouse.

What is happening today is unique. One species of animal life – *Homo sapiens*, ourselves – has achieved such power that all other forms of life are threatened. As our cities spread, they blot out fields and forests that have existed for millions of years. Our high-powered weapons make us the most efficient killers the world has ever known. We destroy our wildlife heritage not only by cutting down forests and draining swamps and ploughing fields to meet our own expanding needs, but by poisoning the environment. We bring death by dumping our wastes into rivers, lakes, and oceans, by pouring factory smoke and automobile exhaust into the air. The great explosion of human population and technology in the last two centuries has produced a correspondingly sharp rise in the number of extinguished species of wildlife. We also hurry the working of extinction by introducing predatory animals such as dogs, cats, foxes, and mongooses into island communities, thus upsetting long-established balances of nature.

On the credit side, man has finally come to show an awareness of his capacity for destruction. He has established zoos and wildlife sanctuaries to preserve what is left of the world's animals; he has passed laws protecting endangered species; he has taken steps to slow the course of obliteration. Although it seems inevitable, if human population continues to grow at its present rate, that within another few hundred years all wildlife will be gone except in special sanctuaries, at least something has been done to delay that melancholy time.

For too many species, though, it is too late to pass protective measures. The final curtain has fallen. In medieval times it was thought wrong to argue that species could become extinct, but the sad proof of that argument is all too obvious to us. The archives of extinction bulge with the records of vanished creatures.

These extinctions are tragic because part of our world has vanished. Human beings once took pleasure in the sight of a sky thronged with passenger pigeons. Men were fascinated by the strangeness of the dodo and the grace of the quagga. When these creatures disappeared, something was subtracted from our lives. We were all diminished by their loss. Whenever an animal becomes extinct, our world is that much poorer.

The death of an entire race of living things is cause for grief. When an individual dies, his friends and relatives mourn, but the race goes on; the passing of one does not mean the disappearance of all. When a race becomes extinct, though, it is like a bright light flickering out. Something unique has disappeared for all eternity. We have only to contemplate how we would feel if some of today's animals were to die out. How dreary the world would be without peacocks and rhinoceroses, without gazelles and eagles, without ostriches, armadillos, aardvarks, alligators, kangaroos!

Perhaps it does not really matter very much that there are no dodos left, or that the great auk is gone. How important is the loss of some odd-looking beast in the history of the world? Not very important at all, possibly. Sooner or later, all animals are bound to die out, anyway. Even if the shotgun had never been invented, the passenger pigeon would eventually have gone the way of the trilobite.

Eventually, yes. But I have never seen a living auk or dodo or passenger pigeon, and neither have you, and we are both a little poorer for not having had the experience. I have been lucky enough to see the oryx and rhinoceros and whooping crane, but that privilege may not be available fifty years from now. A living creature is a unique and irreplaceable work of nature, with a special beauty of its own. To let a species be destroyed is to rob all humanity of the opportunity to experience that unique beauty. It is like constructing a dam to flood a lovely canyon, or demolishing a famous old building, or setting fire to a great painting. Simply from a selfish viewpoint, we are the losers whenever a species becomes extinct, for there is that much less in the world to delight and entertain us.

There is a deeper reason to lament the loss of the quagga and the passenger pigeon and the other animals that have vanished in recent times. We are the custodians of the world we live in. We have an obligation to hand the world on to our descendants in at least as good a condition as it was when we entered it ourselves.

That obligation has generally been ignored. Our ancestors did not keep faith with us; they removed from the world many priceless things that they had no right to destroy. They robbed us of hundreds of types of animals and plants, took away the great forests, spoiled the beauty of the mountains to mine precious minerals. Often they did not understand the long-range consequences of what they were doing, but that does not make it much easier for us to forgive them.

Now the world is in our hands. We could choose to cut down the last redwood tree for its timber, harpoon every whale for its oil, and turn every open tract of land into a row of houses. We could hand on to our successors a world in which all wildlife was gone, every stream was fouled with wastes, and natural beauty was only a memory.

Because we have begun to comprehend our obligations, we are showing more respect for those obligations than our ancestors did. Our parks and zoos and wildlife sanctuaries are postponing the sombre day when the only animal left in the world is man himself. It is only necessary to try to imagine a time when the concrete pavements stretch to the horizons and the trees and beasts are gone, and one can see why the loss of even the tiniest creature is cause for regret.

There is no reason to weep for the trilobites and the dinosaurs. Their disappearance was not our doing. They fell victim to the mighty workings of the laws of nature and were swept to oblivion after enduring for many millions of years. Let us reserve our sorrow for the more recently departed. They were here not so long ago and now are gone, leaving behind them nothing more than bones, stuffed specimens, and a few sketches and tales of travellers.

2

The Dodo

Between the island of Madagascar and the continent of Australia the Indian Ocean stretches for thousands of miles, virtually unbroken by land. In all this wilderness of water the only interruption is a group of three islands along the 20th parallel of southern latitude.

They are known as the Mascarene Islands: Mauritius, Réunion, and Rodriguez. Mauritius, the best known, is a volcanic island about 600 miles east of Madagascar. Réunion lies 106 miles to the south-west of Mauritius, and little Rodriguez 360 miles to the east. They are isolated, lonely places, and were uninhabited by man until the seventeenth century, even though they were, and still are, beautiful and fertile. The Mascarenes have one chief claim to fame: on that group of islands, and nowhere else in the world, lived the bird known as the dodo.

The dodo, a curious-looking, ungainly bird, did not long survive its first contact with humanity. It was discovered in 1598; within less than a century no dodos were left alive. Some scientists began to doubt that it had ever existed, because so little was known about it. The dodo was the first creature whose extinction became a matter of public awareness, and even passed into proverbs. When we say, 'as dead as a dodo', we pay tribute to a lost member of the world's menagerie of odd birds.

The dodo was *very* odd. It was larger than a turkey, round as a sack. Its head was immense and its black bill ended in a great snubbed hook. The plumage was ash-grey in colour, with whitish breast and tail, and yellowish-white wings. Unable to fly, the dodo waddled along on short yellow legs and big splay-toed feet, and when it tried to run it jogged so clumsily that its plump belly scraped the ground. It made its nests on the ground, too, since it had no way to get up into the safety of trees. To us the dodo seems grotesque or comical, just the right sort of bird for Lewis Caroll to have included in *Alice in Wonderland*. The dodo Alice met was solemn, rather dignified, and faintly absurd; it carried a walking stick, spoke in words of many syllables, and when asked a question 'stood for a long time with one finger pressed upon its forehead . . . while the rest waited in silence'. The real dodo, of course, was nothing like Lewis Carroll's, but from what little we know of it, it was a placid, slow-moving creature, loyal to its mate and devoted to its chicks. Such a heavy, awkward, defenceless bird was vulnerable to all enemies. Flightless, unable to run or fight, so feeble of wit that it feared nothing, the dodo could be seized easily by any hunter or any hungry dog.

There were no dogs on the Mascarene Islands, though, until man brought them there. The dodo had no enemies at all before the discovery of the islands. It was incapable of surviving in a hostile environment, but on its own peaceful, remote isle it was in no danger.

Probably the first humans to visit the islands of the dodo were sea-going Arab merchants of the Middle Ages. In the twelfth and thirteenth centuries Arab vessels roved freely and boldly in the Indian Ocean, plying trade routes from the Near East to Africa, India, and China. The three islands are shown on at least one old Arab map. However, there was no business to be transacted on uninhabited islands, and the Arab merchants did not linger there for long.

The European discovery of the Mascarenes came in 1507. The Portuguese had pioneered the sea route from Europe to India via Africa late in the fifteenth century, and now were searching for convenient island bases for the new route. Captain Diogo Fernandes Pereira, sailing

Dodo

eastward from Madagascar, came upon the islands known today as Réunion and Mauritius. He called them Santa Apollonia and Ilha do Cerne. Then he continued towards India, and on the way discovered the island of Rodriguez, which he named Domingo Friz.

The islands thus should be known as the Pereiras, it would seem. Somehow, though, a second Portuguese skipper succeeded in attaching his own name to the group. He was Pedro Mascarenhas, who came that way in 1513, knowing nothing of Pereira's voyage, and rediscovered Mauritius and Réunion. He named the latter island Mascarenhas, after himself, and labelled the whole group the Mascarene Islands. That name still stands, although the designations given by Pereira and Mascarenhas to the individual islands have all been discarded.

These early Portuguese explorers observed that the islands were inhabited only by harmless animals. Probably they noticed a certain fat, stupid-looking, flightless bird, but they said nothing about it in their official accounts of their voyages. The formal discovery of the dodo thus was not made until the end of the sixteenth century, when a Dutch seaman, Admiral Jacob Corneliszoon van Neck, told the world about the unusual bird.

Count Maurice of Nassau, the ruler of the Netherlands, sent Admiral van Neck on a voyage of discovery in 1598 with eight ships. The Dutch fleet found the Mascarenes and landed on the island then known as Ilha do Cerne. Van Neck renamed it Mauritius in honour of his patron, Count Maurice. The Dutch were pleased with the island, whose dark volcanic soil gave promise of great fertility. Exploring it, they noted the rich forests of ebony trees and the abundance of wildlife, including doves, turtles, fish, and huge flocks of a queer bird unlike any that they had ever seen before.

Admiral van Neck's friend and colleague, Admiral Pieter Willem Verhoeven, took a stroll among the dodo nests and, van Neck tell us, was 'pecked mighty hard' for his curiosity. When van Neck's ship returned to Europe in 1599, he had a captive dodo on board. A second dodo arrived six months later aboard one of van Neck's other ships. One of the birds remained in the Netherlands; the other was purchased by Emperor Rudolf II and went to live in Germany.

In 1601 the Journal of van Neck's voyage was published in Dutch by Theodore de Bry, whose books on exploration were widely circulated in Europe. Van Neck described dodos as 'larger than our swans, with huge heads only half covered with skin, as if clothed with a hood. These birds lack wings, in the place of which three or four blackish feathers protrude. The tail consists of a few soft incurved feathers which are ash-coloured. We called these birds *walghvogels* ['disgusting birds'] for the reason that the more and the longer they were cooked, the less soft and more unpalatable their flesh becomes.'

Van Neck and his men may have thought the taste of dodo meat was disgusting, but a second Dutch expedition found the flavour much more enjoyable. In 1601, just as van Neck's account was appearing, a Dutch ship landed at Mauritius and stocked up on *walghvogels* for food. The crewmen captured two dozen of the birds one day, twenty more the next, and sailed away with the larder well stocked with salted fowl. Since there was so much meat on each bird that it provided a night's dinner for half the crew, they were amply supplied for the rest of their voyage.

The Dutch found Mauritius a useful stopping place for ships bound on long journeys. A settlement was soon planted there and the colonists began to grow spices, sugar, pineapple, and other tropical products. They brought along pet dogs, which swiftly learned that they could get a good meal by stealing the eggs from the birds' nests on the ground. The Dutch ships also carried rats; they made their way ashore and soon were merrily feasting on the eggs and the chicks of the slow-moving flightless bird. The settlers themselves made many a good meal out of *walghvogel* meat, as well as laying aside stocks of salted birds to sell to ships that called at their shores. In a short while it became difficult to find any of the birds but no one on Mauritius was worried about that.

In Europe the bird was attracting considerable attention. Several more captive specimens joined the original two. In Germany, Emperor Rudolf's court painter did a portrait in oils of a *walghvogel*. A Dutch painter named Roelandt Savery virtually made a career out of depicting it, producing a number of sketches and paintings. Savery's early paintings of the *walghvogel* apparently were done while observing a live bird, but he seems to have gone on painting it even after he had no model to work from, for his later versions are inaccurate. In error he showed the bird as having duck-like webs between its toes.

The Dutch name, 'disgusting bird', began to give way to the name by which we know the dodo today. Evidently dodo was a word of Portuguese origin. A letter written by an English sailor, Emanuel Altham, about 1628 refers to 'very strange fowles called by ye portingals Do Do'. In Portuguese, *doudo* means 'simpleton', and that was a good description for this lumbering, slow-minded creature.

Travellers calling at Mauritius made a point of viewing the dodo. A good account of the bird was included in the journal of Peter Mundy, an official of the British East India Company and one of the most wide-ranging voyagers since Marco Polo. Mundy visited Mauritius for the first time in March of 1634, and reported seeing 'Dodoes, a strange kinde of a fowle, twice as bigg as a Goose, that can neither flye nor swymm, beinge Cloven footed; a wonder how it should come thither, there being none such in any part of the world yett to be found'. He noted having earlier seen two dodos that had been brought from Mauritius to India as pets.

Calling at Mauritius again four years later on his way home from China, Mundy looked for dodos once more. But by 1638 they were becoming scarce on the island. 'We now mett with None,' he jotted in his diary. 'As I remember they are as bigge bodied as great Turkeyes, covered with Downe, having little hanguing wings like shortt sleeves, alltogether unuseffull to Fly withal, or any way with them to helpe themselves.'

At least a dozen dodos had reached Europe alive by this time – one to Italy, one to Germany, several to England, and eight or nine to Holland, both males and females. One dodo was put on public display in London. Among those who saw it was a certain Sir Hamon Lestrange, who wrote, 'About 1638, as I walked London streets, I saw the picture of a strange fowle hong out upon a cloth, and myselfe with one or two more then in company went in to see it. It was kept in a chamber, and was a great fowle somewhat bigger than the largest Turkey Cock. . . . The keeper called it a Dodo.' He watched it swallowing pebbles as big as nutmegs.

This dodo or another one was bought after its death by John Tradescant, an English naturalist and collector. He had it stuffed and put among his specimens of unusual creatures. The catalogue of his collection, published in 1656, lists 'a Dodar from the Island of Mauritius. . . . It is not able to flie being so big.' When Tradescant died, his collection of stuffed birds was transferred to the Ashmolean Museum at Oxford. The stuffed dodo took up residence there in 1683.

It was then two years since anyone had seen a dodo alive on Mauritius.

An Englishman named Benjamin Harry, visiting Mauritius in 1681, was the last to see a living dodo. When anybody bothered to look for one again, twelve years later, no dodos could be found. The dogs and the rats and the Dutch settlers had wiped them out in less than a century. Having evolved in an environment without a single enemy, the dodo had been unable to withstand the constant raids of man and beast, and had dwindled to the

Mauritius Dodo, after a seventeenth-century drawing

vanishing point. By 1750 the inhabitants of Mauritius did not even remember that there had been such a bird.

The various live dodos brought back to Europe had all died also, and none had left descendants. Nothing remained to tell the world that the dodo had ever existed except a badly stuffed and rather mangy specimen in an Oxford museum. The moth-eaten Oxford dodo looked so shabby that the curator of the museum decided in 1755 to throw it away. Someone removed the head and one foot of the specimen and saved them; the rest was burned as rubbish. In that way the only dodo in any museum was lost.

The scientists of the eighteenth century made the overdue discovery that a unique creature had been allowed to perish virtually without trace. Not only the dodo of Mauritius was gone for ever, but also two related birds of the other two Mascarene Islands. Rodriguez and Réunion had also had dodo-like birds – but they, too, were extinct by the time any serious study of this family began.

The dodo of Mauritius had been a dark-coloured bird. On neighbouring Réunion, the dodos were yellowish-white, with black wingtips. They differed in a number of other ways from the Mauritius bird. Evolution had taken three different paths with these flightless fat birds of the Mascarenes. Perhaps in the distant past there had been only one type of dodo on all three islands, but since there was no contact between the widely separated islands, each dodo had developed in its own characteristic way.

No one paid much attention to the 'white dodo' of Réunion until it was extinct. Réunion is larger than Mauritius, but much more mountainous, and it did not attract settlers. It still wore its old Portuguese name of Mascarenhas when an English captain named Castleton visited it in 1613. Twelve years later, a member of the crew published an account of Castleton's voyage and described 'a great fowl of the bigness of a Turkie, very fat, and so short-winged that they cannot flie, being white, and in a manner tame'. Clearly this was a dodo of a different colour. In 1619 a Dutch traveller, Willem Bontekoe van Hoorn, spent three weeks there and described a bird he called the *dad-eersen*, which obviously was the same kind Castleton had seen. Bontekoe van Hoorn observed that the bird was so fat it could not run.

No one else who saw the Réunion dodo alive set down a record of the fact. In 1638 a French ship arrived at the island, claimed it for France, and replaced its Portuguese name with the present one. French settlers landed and proceeded to hunt the local wildlife into extinction. A

White Dodo, after a seventeenth-century drawing

couple of white dodos were shipped to Europe, one about 1640 and one around 1685. They were painted by Dutch artists. Then, very quietly, the white dodo disappeared from existence. The fact that it was extinct was not noticed until 1801, when a survey of Réunion's animal population failed to find it, but it probably had perished more than a century earlier.

The third of the Mascarene Islands – Rodriguez – had its own special variety of the dodo. Rodriguez is small, only ten miles long and four miles broad, and few ships ever bothered to land at it. Pereira visited it in 1507 and Mascarenhas saw it, though he did not go ashore, six years later. After several changes of name it became known as Rodriguez, and that name remained even after the French took possession of it in 1638.

The first detailed exploration of Rodriguez came about through accident. Late in the seventeenth century there was religious strife in France between the Huguenots, or Protestants, and the dominant Catholics. Many Huguenots were massacred for their beliefs, and others were driven into exile. A group of these Huguenot refugees reached the Netherlands in 1689 and asked the Dutch to provide them with some distant land where they could settle in peace.

The Dutch suggested Réunion. In theory that was French property, but it was believed that the French had withdrawn from the island. In 1690 a Dutch ship carrying these French Protestants sailed for the Mascarenes. The voyage was an arduous one, and many of the Huguenots fell ill. When the ship stopped at the Cape of Good Hope for provisions, they learned to their dismay that Réunion was still occupied by the French after all. The Huguenots could not go there, obviously, nor could they settle on Mauritius, which was a Dutch colony. Just one island in the vicinity remained, lonely Rodriguez.

There were only eight Huguenots in the group, led by a man in his fifties named François Leguat. They spent about two years on Rodriguez. Life on the rocky little island was harsh, and the unhappy colonists finally built a boat and made the risky journey to Mauritius. There they were seized by the Dutch governor, who did not want them on his island and banished them to a small rocky islet offshore, where they were imprisoned for three years, and then shipped, still as prisoners, to Java. After many improbable hardships Leguat and two of his companions, the only survivors of the original group of Huguenots, gained their freedom and returned to Europe in 1698. Leguat settled in England, and in 1708 the journal of his adventurous travels was published.

He showed himself to have been a good observer of natural history. Much of his book was devoted to the plants and animals he saw on Rodriguez. 'Of all the Birds in the Island,' he wrote, 'the most Remarkable is that which goes by the Name of the Solitary, because 'tis very seldom seen in Company, tho' there are abundance of them. The Feathers of the Males are of a brown, grey Colour: the Feet and Beak are like a Turkeys, but a little more crooked. They have scarce any Tail, but their Hindpart cover'd with Feathers is Roundish, like the Crupper of a Horse, they are taller than Turkeys. Their Neck is straight, and a little longer in proportion than a Turkeys, when it lifts up his Head. Its Eye is black and lively, and its Head without Comb ... They never fly, their Wings are too little to support the weight of their Bodies; they serve only to beat themselves, and flutter when they call one another.'

Leguat declared: ' 'Tis very hard to catch it in the Woods, but easie in open Places, because we run faster than they, and sometimes we approach them without much Trouble. From March to September they are extremely fat, and taste admirably well, especially while they are young, some of the Males weigh forty-five Pound.'

The female solitaries, Leguat said, 'are wonderfully beautiful, some fair, some brown,' and 'no one Feather is

stragling from the other all over their Bodies, they being
very careful to adjust themselves, and make them all
even with their Beaks ... When these Birds build their
Nests, they choose a clean Place, gather together some
Palm-Leaves for that purpose, and heap them up a foot
and a half high from the Ground, on which they sit.
They never lay but one Egg [at a time], which is much
bigger than that of a Goose. The Male and Female both
cover it in their turns, and the young is not hatch'd till at
seven Weeks end: All the while they are sitting upon it,
or bringing up their young one, which is not able to provide for its self in several Months.'

Leguat's description of the habits of the solitary provides one more reason why these birds became extinct.
Producing only one egg each season, they were slow to
breed, and could never make up the loss in numbers
caused by the introduction of predatory animals to their
islands.

Rodriguez had few callers after the Huguenot exiles.
Some English sailors stayed there until about 1707, and a
French expedition surveyed the island in 1725. A small
settlement was founded. The French inhabitants of Rodriguez supported themselves by catching fish that were
sold on Mauritius and Réunion. In 1761 a French
scientific expedition came to Rodriguez to make astro-
nomical observations. A member of this party, the Abbé
Pingré, had read Leguat's book and went looking for solitaries. He found some of the flightless birds, but he seems
to have been the last to see them alive.

By the middle of the eighteenth century the dodos of
Mauritius, the white dodos of Réunion, and the solitaries of Rodriguez were all extinct. They were virtually
forgotten as well. Scientists had given them Latin names
and then had thrust them out of mind. The dodo of

Mauritius had been dubbed *Raphus cucullatus*, which means 'cuckoo-like bird with seams'. The dodo is not really cuckoo-like, and it does not have seams, so the great naturalist and classifier of the eighteenth century, Carolus Linnaeus, gave it a more proper name. He called it *Didus ineptus*, 'clumsy dodo'. That name was used for a long

Solitary

time, until someone remembered the earlier one. By the accepted laws of science, the first Latin name given is the one that must be used, and so the dodo is once again known by its silly designation as a 'cuckoo with seams'.

As for the Réunion dodo, that was clearly a relative of the Mauritius bird, and therefore was placed in the same genus, or group as *Didus ineptus*. Because it was a different species of that genus, it was named *Didus borbonicus*, in honour of the Bourbons, the royal family of France. (Considering what a dodo looks like, it was a dubious honour.) No one was quite sure if or how the solitary of Rodriguez was related to the other two, so it went into a genus of its own as *Pezophaps solitarius*, 'The solitary walking pigeon'.

By 1800, though, some authorities on natural history had come to doubt that any of these birds had ever existed. What proof was there? The head and foot of a dodo at Oxford, yes; but that was not enough. No skeletons were in any scientific collection. No stuffed specimens were known. The reports of the early voyagers might be in error; plenty of imaginary beasts like unicorns and dragons had been reported by gullible travellers, so perhaps the dodo, too, was a figment of someone's imagination. The available paintings and sketches of dodos made in the seventeenth century did not help the situation. They contradicted each other in too many details. Besides, it was hard to believe that such a ridiculous-looking creature could be authentic.

The doubts grew so strong that in 1828 an Oxford zoologist named J. S. Duncan went over all the evidence and wrote a paper proving that there really had been a dodo. His work aroused interest in Mauritius, which by this time had passed through the hands of the Dutch and the French and had become a British possession. Three educated men of the island formed a Society of Natural History and went looking for dodo bones. They did not have much success. However, one member of the society went to Rodriguez and managed to unearth in caves some large, unfamiliar bones, which were sent to Europe for study. The scientific verdict was that these were the remains of Leguat's solitary, so that bird, at least, was shown to have been genuine.

The search for dodo remains continued. George Clark, a native of Mauritius interested in natural history, led the quest. When nothing came to light on the island, Clark developed an ingenious theory to explain the shortage of bones. The soil of Mauritius, he said, is not suitable for the deposit of fossil remains. Much of the island is covered by thick clay or by volcanic lava. The heavy tropical rains, striking this hard floor, would wash any bones away before they could safely be buried in the earth.

Where, Clark asked himself, were the bones likely to go when the rain swept them away?

Three rivers met and ran into the sea near the town of Mahébourg, forming a muddy, marshy delta. Clark reasoned that if any dodo bones had been washed into any of these rivers, they would ultimately have come to rest in the mud of the delta. In 1863 he hired some labourers and began to excavate the marshes. Sure enough, a large number of dodo bones came to light. The scattered bones were assembled into complete skeletons and shipped to museums in many parts of the world. Thanks to the work of George Clark, a mounted dodo skeleton can be seen at the American Museum of Natural History in New York, and at the Smithsonian Institution in Washington. The Natural History Museum in London, the Western Australian Museum in Perth and the East London Museum in South Africa all have models of the dodo made up to look like stuffed specimens. The South African Museum also has what is claimed to be a dodo egg.

The mystery of the dodo's existence had been solved. Now it was indisputable that three species of closely related flightless birds had lived on the Mascarenes until a catastrophic collision with the human race doomed them in the seventeenth and eighteenth centuries. The grey dodo of Mauritius had been the first to go, then its white-feathered cousin of Réunion, and finally the brown solitary of Rodriguez. By studying the skeletons found in the middle of the nineteenth century, scientists were able to confirm that the dodo had been every bit as grotesque-looking as the paintings and travellers' descriptions indicated.

One thing remained to fit the Mascarene dodos into the family of birds. The early attempts at doing this had been unhappy ones. Leguat, in describing the birds of the islands, had also spoken of a bird he called a 'giant', which he said was six feet high, with long legs and a tiny body. No one is quite sure what this bird really was, though it apparently was a kind of crane or heron. But one of Leguat's contemporaries called it a type of ostrich. Through a weird process of confusion, the idea spread that Leguat's solitary was also an ostrich which simply happened to have short legs. So when Linnaeus drew up his classification of the animal kingdom in the eighteenth century, he put the dodos and their kin down as short-legged ostriches.

That was obviously absurd, and in 1835 a French zoologist made a new suggestion that was even more preposterous. The dodo, he said, was a type of vulture. Now, the big hooked beak of the dodo might remind some people of a vulture's bill, but otherwise it was laughable to compare the plump, waddling dodo with the lean, swift-winged vulture. Nevertheless for a few years the dodo was accepted in the vulture tribe, simply on the basis of its beak.

Then someone took the trouble to look up the accounts of van Neck, Leguat, and the others who had seen the Mascarene birds while they were still in existence. These observers were agreed that the dodos had been vegetarians, and not birds of prey like the vultures at all. So the dodo was taken from the vulture family and thrust into one classification after another. It was grouped with the penguin, with the snipe, even with such lordly, graceful birds as the ibis and the crane.

An English ornithologist named Hugh Strickland disagreed with all these suggestions. In the 1840s he began to study the dodos with a fresh viewpoint. No skeletons were yet available, but he did the next best thing, and travelled to Holland to examine the dodo paintings of Roelandt Savery. Strickland published a slim book called *The Dodo and Its Kindred* in 1848, putting forth a new idea. The dodo, he said, was a giant dove which had settled on the Mascarenes long ago. It had grown heavy and had lost the ability to fly. Because the islands lacked any dangerous animals, the dodo had been able to survive there as a kind of living fossil, though it could not have endured life anywhere else.

The experts were amused. Doves, relatives of the pigeons, were lithe, gentle, attractive birds. How could the awkward dodo, with its strange hooked beak, possibly belong to the dove family?

Strickland died in a railway accident in 1853, and so never saw the triumph of his theory. Soon after his death, explorers on the Pacific island of Samoa discovered a large, powerful bird with a thick, hooked beak. It appeared to be a big dove, but its beak marked it as a relative of the dodo. The dove of Samoa appeared to occupy a middle position between the familiar doves of Europe and the flightless dodo of the Mascarenes.

Now the evolutionary pattern was clear. Millions of years ago, the ancestors of today's doves and pigeons had been big birds with prominent beaks. One branch of the family had evolved towards the peaceful doves and pigeons. Another branch of the family, settling in the islands of the Pacific, had retained some of the ancestral characteristics. And a third branch had made its way to the isolated Mascarene Islands, where life was tranquil and no enemies existed. Since it was unnecessary for the Mascarene birds to fly, they gradually lost the use of their wings. As they adapted to life on the ground, they grew bigger and clumsier, until they could barely get around at all. When men came to the Mascarenes, bringing with them dogs, pigs, and rats, the awkward birds were doomed.

The dodo skeletons that George Clark found in the 1860s proved the Strickland theory. The dodo, bizarre though it looked, was nothing but an oversized dove, and an ideal candidate for speedy extinction.

3

The Aurochs and
the Bison

Rudyard Kipling's poem, 'The Story of Ung', tells of an artist of the Stone Age who learned the secret of carving images. His fellow tribesmen came to see what he had made, and were impressed:

Pleased was his tribe with that image – came in their hundreds to scan –
Handled it, smelt it, and grunted: 'Verily, this is a man!
Thus do we carry our lances – thus is a war-belt slung.
Ay, it is even as we are. Glory and honour to Ung!'
Later he pictured an aurochs – later he pictured a bear –
Pictured the sabre-toothed tiger dragging a man to his lair –
Pictured the mountainous mammoth, hairy, abhorrent, alone –
Out of the love that he bore them, scribing them clearly on bone.

The woolly mammoth, the ferocious sabre-toothed tiger, and the bear are long since gone from Europe. They died out fifteen or twenty thousand years ago. But what of the other prehistoric animal of Kipling's poem, the mysterious aurochs? What kind of beast was that?

It was one of the ancestors of modern cattle – a long-horned wild ox that roamed the forests of Europe until three hundred years ago. A survivor of the time when the men of Europe were skin-clad huntsmen who painted pictures on the walls of caves, the aurochs lived on into a more civilized era, and civilization wiped it out.

Kipling was wrong, though, when in his poem he listed the aurochs among the animals hunted during the deep freeze of the glacial period. He described his prehistoric men attacking the aurochs 'when the red snow reeks of the flight', but actually the aurochs was not present in Europe during the worst years of the ice ages. The only member of the cattle family that endured the cold was the aurochs' relative, the bison.

Finding the proper place for the aurochs in the cattle family has long been a troublesome matter. For more than two thousand years it has been confused with the bison and the buffalo. The bison and buffalo, for that matter, have long been confused with each other.

The buffalo has always been a warm-weather animal. It belongs to the genus *Bubalus* and is found in tropical countries from Egypt to the Philippines. It is a large, clumsy animal with heavy horns that curve backwards and inwards. The buffalo's coarse hair lies flat on the body, giving it a smooth appearance. In the wild, it spends much of its time wallowing in mud and shallow water. The African buffalo is a different species, *Syncerus caffer*, found south of the Sahara. Buffaloes never existed in the wild in Europe or North America. In Roman times, some buffaloes were introduced into Italy from Africa for agricultural uses.

The cold-weather member of the cattle family is the bison, which, together with the aurochs and domestic cattle, is classed in the genus *Bos*. The bison is a shaggy-furred, hump-backed beast with a large lowered head and short, sharp, upcurving horns. It originated in the Himalayas, Persia, and southern Siberia, and during the ice ages gradually entered Europe. Its thick fur shielded it against the cold. One species of bison, *Bos bison*, found its way into North America from Asia and thrived on the western plains. This big, brownish-black animal was the 'buffalo' that Buffalo Bill and other nineteenth-century hunters slew in such great numbers. The European species of bison, *Bos bonasus*, remained in Europe even after the ice ages gave way to a time of warmer climate. Less massive than its American cousin, the European bison preferred to live in forests, while the American form chose open prairies.

The shaggy, short-horned European bison was quite different from the aurochs, which had extremely long horns and short hair. The aurochs, *Bos primigenius* ('the ancestor of cattle'), was distantly related to the oxen of the tropics, such as the gaur of India, the gayal of Burma, and the banteng of Malaya. It looked like a bigger and longer-horned version of the modern domestic cattle that are descended from it. Late in prehistoric times, when the glaciers had begun to thaw, the aurochs left its homeland North Africa and Asia and migrated into Europe. It is portrayed only in the most recent of the cave paintings of the ice age, executed about fifteen thousand years ago.

There was really no reason to confuse the urus, as the Romans called the aurochs, with the bonasus, or bison. Yet they were confused all the time.

One of the first writers to mention the aurochs was Julius Caesar, who discovered it when he marched westwards in 58 BC to conquer the Gauls and the other wild tribes of what are now France and Germany. Caesar was familiar with the bison, which had often been captured in the forests and brought to Rome to fight with gladiators in the arenas. But he had never seen the aurochs until he came to the Hercynian forest of Germany.

This forest, in a mountainous region north of the Danube River, was of immense size. Caesar wrote: 'No western German claims to have reached its eastern extremity, even after travelling for two months, or to have heard where it ends. The forest is known to contain many kinds of animals not seen elsewhere, some of which seem worthy of mention because they differ greatly from those found in other countries.'

Aurochs

Among these strange beasts was the urus, 'an animal somewhat smaller than the elephant, with the appearance, colour, and shape of a bull. They are very strong and agile, and attack every man and beast they catch sight of. The natives take great pains to trap them in pits, and then kill them. This arduous sport toughens the young men and keeps them in training; and those who kill the largest number exhibit the horns in public to show what they have done, and earn high praise. It is impossible to domesticate or tame the urus, even if it is caught young. The horns are much larger than those of our oxen, and of quite different shape and appearance. The Germans prize them greatly; they mount the rims with silver and use them as drinking-cups at their grandest banquets.'

Caesar was careful to distinguish the urus from the domestic bull (*Bos taurus*) and from *Bos bonasus*, the hump-backed, shaggy wild bison. But when the great Roman naturalist, Pliny the Elder, wrote his *Natural History* about a century later, he expressed his annoyance at those who insisted on blurring the distinctions between aurochs and bison, bison and buffalo: 'Germany . . . had not many animals,' he wrote, 'though it has some very fine kinds of wild oxen: the bison, which has a mane, and the urus, possessed of remarkable strength and swiftness. To these, the vulgar, in their ignorance, have given the name of *bubalus* [buffalo]: whereas that animal is really produced in Africa.'

The forests of Europe began to disappear as population grew. Such wild animals of the woods as the lynx, the wolf, and the elk became rare. Both the urus and the bison were severely reduced in numbers. Latin dropped from use, too; the urus became known in the Middle Ages as an *aurochs* in Germany, as a *thur* in Poland and other eastern countries. The wild bison now was called a *subr* in Poland, a *wisent* in Germany.

Both animals still were mentioned frequently by European writers. In the *Nibelungenlied*, a German epic poem of medieval times, the hero, Siegfried, is described as slaying first a bison and an elk, then 'four strong aurochs'. But as other Siegfrieds duplicated those heroic deeds, all the large forest animals of Europe were killed off. The aurochs and the bison became so rare that men forgot that they were different animals. The Swiss naturalist, Conrad Gesner, writing in the sixteenth century, told of seeing an aurochs' horn six feet long on display in the cathedral of Strasbourg, and declared that the aurochs 'is incorrectly described as the German wisent'. The artist who illustrated Gesner's book, though, was obviously not certain which was which; he drew an animal with the body of an aurochs and the short horns and beard of a bison. About the same time, an Austrian artist named Augustin Hirsfogel published woodcuts of the aurochs and the bison. The picture of the aurochs was captioned, 'I am a urus, called by the Poles a thur, by the Germans an aurochs, and by the ignorant a bison.' Above the bison's portrait was a line, 'I am a bison, called by the Poles a subr, by the Germans a wisent or dam-thier, and by the ignorant an aurochs.'

By the sixteenth century, the only animals of either kind that remained were found on the large estates of the European nobility. The bison was fairly common on these game preserves, but the aurochs, which had been heavily hunted for its long, ornamental horns, could be seen in just a few places. One of them was the private park of Duke Albrecht of Prussia in Königsberg, where in 1563 a writer named Gratiani viewed both the aurochs and the bison, and even was treated to dinner of aurochs veal. About the same time, in Poland, regulations were issued making it illegal to keep the *subr* (bison) and the *thur* (aurochs) in the same park, since the two scarce types of cattle disliked each other and did battle whenever they met.

The aristocrats of Europe enjoyed hunting the aurochs in their lordly forests. It was a pleasure they refused to give up, even when it became obvious that hardly any of the long-horned oxen remained. The peasants, too, made a practice of slipping into the private parks to poach, and it did not matter to them that the aurochs was extremely rare. A good steak, after all, was a good steak.

Before long there was only one place in the world where the aurochs still could be found: the game preserve of Jaktorowka in Poland. No hunting was allowed there. The keepers kept a careful record of births and deaths in the herd. Despite their best efforts, poachers kept raiding the preserve. In 1565 only thirty head of aurochs remained. By 1602 there were just four. In 1620 a single aurochs was left, an elderly cow. The keepers guarded her with care, but nothing could be done to save the species. When she died in 1627, the aurochs became extinct. Man had succeeded at last in exterminating this magnificent wild ox.

European Bison

The fate of the wisent, or European bison, was nearly as sad. It had always been more common than the aurochs, and as recently as 1534 great herds of them ranged the forests of Hungary, Germany, and Poland. An account written in that year declared, 'The wild oxen live in hordes in Hungarian Szeklerland and do much damage, also killing with their feet men and women who go into the forest. Therefore great ox hunts are held ... when many gentlemen and nobles gather together and there is also much hard drinking.' These lively festivals brought the extinction of the bison of Hungary by 1800.

In Prussia, then an independent kingdom and now part of East Germany, bison were kept in a royal preserve. Frederick I of Prussia led hunting parties against this dwindling herd as late as 1701. So few remained, though, that the hunts ceased. A census of Prussian bison taken in 1726 showed 117 head. Poachers continued to prey on them. In 1740, when King Frederick the Great came to the Prussian throne, only 40 bison were left. At the king's command these survivors were protected from poachers, but a severe blizzard in the winter of 1742 killed most of them, and the last Prussian bison died in 1755.

Bison herds in Lithuania and Poland still existed, but disease and harsh winters thinned the herds, and the desire of the European aristocrats to hunt rare animals did further damage. In 1752 the Queen of Saxony shot twenty fenced-in bison in a single day, and there were other hunts that produced thirty or more kills in one afternoon. By 1800 the Lithuanian bison were gone and the only Polish ones that survived were some three hundred head in the forest of Bialowieza.

When this part of Poland became Russian territory in 1802, Tsar Alexander I took a dramatic step to save the bison herd. He declared the entire eight hundred square miles of the Bialowieza forest a protected area, and forced all the peasants living there to move elsewhere so there would be no danger from poachers. The Tsar also was the proprietor of the only other herd of European bison, about a thousand animals living in the mountains of the Caucasus, in south-western Russia.

The well-protected Bialowieza bison steadily increased in numbers. In 1813 there were 350 of them; by 1822, they totalled 650 head, and the bison census of 1846 listed 1,095. The peak was reached in 1857, when there were 1,898 head. But disease, hungry poachers, and rugged weather began to reduce the herd. Only 874 bison were alive in 1863, and a mere 479 by 1891. The downward trend was reversed for a while, so that the herd numbered 737 in 1914. That was the year the First World War began.

During the war, Russian and Polish soldiers passing through the Bialowieza forest killed bison for meat. Poachers took care of the rest. The last of the Bialowieza bison was shot on 19 February 1921.

The bison of the Caucasus had met with a similar fate. A count made between 1909 and 1911 showed about seven hundred bison in the main herd, with less than a hundred others in several smaller herds. During the upheavals of the First World War, all these animals were killed. Regiments of the Soviet army conducted hunts with machine guns in the Caucasian preserve until none were left.

At the end of the war, less than fifty European bison existed. Most of them were old, and many were bulls. Extinction seemed almost certain. These survivors were widely scattered: two small herds in Sweden, one herd in the Budapest zoo, another on a private estate in Germany, and single animals in nine or ten European zoos. The largest herd – about twenty bison – lived in England on the estate of the Duke of Bedford, a collector of rare animals.

A determined effort was made to keep the wisent from going the way of the aurochs. Through international co-operation the remaining bison were mated and bred. By 1928 there were sixty bison, and ten years later there were a hundred. The Second World War brought new hardships to these animals; at the end of the war, only seventy bison remained. However, these have now increased to about eight hundred head, and the extinction of the European bison no longer seems imminent. Good-sized herds now exist in several countries. They have even been introduced once again into the Bialowieza forest of Poland.

The American bison, incorrectly called the buffalo by so many people, suffered a similar fate. When the white man first came to America, incredible millions of these huge, superb animals lived on the western prairies. To the Indians who hunted them, they were the source of every necessity. Bison meat was food; bison hides became moccasins, robes, wigwams, and canoes. The short curving horns were made into drinking cups and the bones were fashioned into a variety of tools and weapons. Though the Indians hunted the bison for centuries, they were so few in number that they made no dent in the enormous herds.

A traveller named Hepword Dickson, who went west just after the Civil War, viewed the prairies when they still were the home of 60 million bison. He wrote:

'The black, shaggy beasts continued to thunder past us in handfuls, in groups, in masses, in whole armies; for forty hours in succession we never lost sight of them, thousands upon thousands, tens of thousands upon tens of thousands, a numberless multitude of untamed creatures, whose meat, as we thought, would be sufficient to supply the wigwams of the Indians to all eternity.'

The Indians, though, stood in the white man's way. They fought back when he tried to run his railways through their hunting grounds. Late in the nineteenth century a war of extermination was launched by the

American Bison

United States against the Indians of the west. An important feature of this war was a deliberate campaign of bison slaughter. Wiping out the bison would doom the Indians as well.

In 1871 professional hunters went west and began to destroy the herds. Thousands of them camped on the plains, each man shooting as many as fifty or sixty bison a day. The hides and meat were allowed to go to waste; huge areas of the prairie were littered with the decaying carcasses of the animals. The most famous of these hunters was William Cody, 'Buffalo Bill', who boasted that he had personally killed 4,280 'buffalos' in a year and a half. In his autobiography he told rousing tales of his adventures, and his feats won him world-wide fame. A typical Cody enterprise was his bet with Billy Comstock, another hunter: 'The wager was five hundred dollars a side, and the man who should kill the greater number of buffaloes from horseback [within eight hours] was to be declared the winner.' While an admiring tourist party of 'about a hundred gentlemen and ladies' who had come out from St Louis to watch the sport looked on, Comstock and Cody went to work. By late afternoon Buffalo Bill had slain sixty-nine 'buffalos', Comstock only forty-six. 'The referees declared me the winner of the match,' Cody wrote, 'as well as the champion buffalo hunter of the plains.'

The transcontinental line of the new Union Pacific Railway became a boundary for the bison herds. By 1875, the 3 million bison south of the railway had been reduced to a hundred thousand, and these were slaughtered within the next three years. The much larger herds north of the railway took longer to destroy. Yet by 1885 these millions of bison were gone.

Startled by the efficiency of the campaign, some conservationists finally succeeded in getting the public to see that a great tragedy had taken place. If the unlimited hunt continued, the last few bison soon would be dead. State officials began to collect the scattered survivors of the massacre. One state found ten bison, another four, another turned up a herd of twenty-five. These were put in protected reserves.

Congress officially ended the butchery in 1889. A last roundup was held and eighty-nine wild bison were gathered. These were the only survivors of a population of 60 million on the prairies. In addition, about five hundred American bison were safe behind fences in Yellowstone National Park, and some five hundred more were protected in a Canadian national park. Since many of these bison were old and past the time of fertility, it seemed almost certain that extinction was near for the species. A serious epidemic or two, a bad winter on the prairies, and the last survivors would die.

Dedicated individuals saw that this did not happen. They were led by William T. Hornaday of the New York Zoological Park, who founded the American Bison Society to protect and preserve the remaining animals. Hornaday's crusade raised money to establish bison reservations, to provide shelter and winter fodder for the animals, and to bring about matings. When President Theodore Roosevelt gave the organization his support in 1905, many Americans joined the effort. In that year there were 1,697 bison in existence. By 1908 the population was 2,047, and it reached the 3,000 mark in 1913. Today the American bison is out of danger. There are some 15,000 in Canada and 5,000 more in the United States. Bison herds can be seen in several of the national parks and there are bison in every major zoo. Like its European cousin, the American bison was pulled back from the brink of extinction at the last moment.

An interesting project is under way today in Germany: an attempt to bring back the long-lost aurochs through selective breeding. Cattle experts in Munich have chosen modern breeds of cattle that closely resemble the aurochs, picking those with the longest horns, the smoothest black coats, and the most powerful bodies. They hope to breed for these aurochs traits until they have produced a herd of cattle displaying the characteristics of the ancestral wild form.

The results so far are encouraging. It seems that they will succeed in breeding an animal that looks like the aurochs. But it will not *be* an aurochs. The last aurochs died in 1627, and no scientific magic can bring it to life again. The aurochs is gone for ever.

4

Steller's Sea Cow

The legend of the mermaid goes back to ancient times. Three thousand years ago, the Assyrians worshipped a god who was half man, half fish. A Phoenician goddess was a woman from the waist up, a fish from the thighs down. Pliny the Elder in his *Natural History* reported sightings of mermaids. Sailors venturing to distant oceans brought home stories of beguiling creatures with womanly bodies and long fishy tails.

When Henry Hudson tried to sail eastward to China in 1609, he, too, encountered a mermaid. Hudson was attempting what was known as the North-east Passage – through the Arctic Ocean north of Scandinavia and Russia to the eastern tip of Siberia, and down into the Pacific. The journey through the polar seas was a hard one, and Hudson got no farther east than the big double island of Novaya Zemlya before turning back. In those chilly waters he spied a number of seals and walruses, and on a June evening one of his men, looking overboard, caught sight of a mermaid.

Hudson tells us that the man called to a fellow crewman to see, 'and by that time she was come close to the ship's side, looking earnestly on the men. A little after, a sea came and overturned her. From the navel upward, her back and breasts were like a woman's, as they say that saw her; her body as big as one of us, her skin very white, and long hair hanging down behind, of colour black. In her going down they saw her tail, which was like the tail of a porpoise, speckled like a mackerel. Their names that saw her were Thomas Hilles and Robert Rayner.'

Other seamen, too, claimed to have sighted mermaids – in Florida, the West Indies, off the coast of South America, and in the great rivers of Brazil, Venezuela, and Guiana. Mermaids were common in the seventeenth-century seas, evidently. But the Arctic mermaid of Henry Hudson was the only one ever discovered in cold waters. All the rest were tropical mermaids.

In the eighteenth century scientists provided a prosaic explanation for these wondrous creatures. The supposed mermaids were actually large seagoing mammals known as sirenians. There is nothing very attractive about a sirenian; they are bulky, blubbery beasts with wrinkled hides and whiskery faces. But perhaps a sailor who had not seen a woman for many months might mistake a sirenian for a fair damsel of the sea, especially if the sailor happened to be near-sighted and the sirenian was a considerable distance from the ship.

Two types of sirenians were known. An animal named the dugong inhabited the shores of the Mediterranean, the Red Sea, and the Indian Ocean, and had been seen by mariners for thousands of years. Dugongs, massive animals ten to twelve feet long and weighing nearly a ton, are slow-moving aquatic beasts that feed on vegetation. The front limbs have become flippers, and the hind limbs have fused to form a tail. Like seals, dolphins, whales, and other water-dwelling mammals, dugongs probably once were land creatures that were tailored by evolution for life in the sea. Although they can remain submerged for a long time, filling their lungs with air and closing their nostrils with special valves, they must eventually come to the surface to breathe.

Since dugongs are mammals, they nurse their young, and this is probably the root of the mermaid legend. Dugongs have two breasts, placed approximately in the same region of the chest as human breasts. The sight of a female dugong at a distance, with her pink skin and her human-looking breasts, may well have given rise to stories of mermaids.

Manatee

The exploration of the New World produced a second kind of sirenian, the manatee. These are fresh-water animals, while dugongs prefer the sea. They move slowly along the floors of rivers and lakes, grazing on water plants. Like dugongs, they have flippers and tails and a pair of breasts. But no sailor was likely to mistake one of those grey-black beasts for a lovely woman if he saw it at close range. A species of manatee discovered in a West African river in the eighteenth century received this description:

'Its face is as ugly as its name is beautiful, if one can call it a face at all. Its mouth – or rather its snout – is incredibly wide, has cleft lips and veritable tusks. The bulging eyes protrude from the sockets, the nose looks as though it had been squashed. Two heavy breasts hang down over its bristly belly. It has two arms with five three-jointed fingers on each hand, but the fingers are joined together by a strong, pliable web as in ducks. From the waist down the creature is a fish with a forked tail. Its thick, strong skin is so elastic that it can hide its young therein as in a cloak.'

The identification of the dugong and the manatee as the mermaids seen by so many sailors seem to put the mermaid legend to rest. But one question remained unanswered. If sirenians lived only in warm climates, what was the creature that Henry Hudson's men had seen in the Arctic in 1609?

That question was not settled until 1742. A remarkable scientific expedition – and an even more remarkable scientist – found the probable answer.

Tsar Peter the Great, when he came to the throne of Russia in 1689, found himself the ruler of a vast but backward realm. Few Russians could read or write. The nation was poor despite its great natural resources. While Europe had progressed, Russia had slept. Peter the Great set into motion a violent wave of change and reform. One of his projects was a complete exploration of Siberia, Russia's enormous Asiatic sector. 'Everything shall be discovered that has not yet been discovered,' the Tsar commanded.

In 1718 Peter sent out an expedition to explore the Kamchatka peninsula of eastern Siberia. He wanted to know 'whether Asia and America are united', and ordered his captains to 'go not only north and south but east and west'. After a three-year cruise, the expedition returned to Moscow in 1722 without having actually determined the geography of Kamchatka. It still was not known if Siberia joined the north-western tip of North America.

Late in 1724 Peter drew up orders for a new expedition. He selected as its commander a Danish officer, Vitus Bering. Bering, who was born in 1681, had gone to sea as a boy, and had made voyages to the East and West Indies before enrolling in the Russian navy at the age of twenty-three. Tsar Peter, founding his navy from scratch, had hired capable sailors from all over Europe, since there were few native Russian seamen at that time. Bering displayed his courage and endurance in many voyages under Russian service, seeing military action in a war against Sweden.

A month after picking Bering for the expedition, Tsar Peter died. The voyage proceeded anyway, and Bering spent several years exploring eastern Siberia. After a strenuous reconnaissance of that bleak country, he returned to Russia in 1730. Bering had tried to get a clear idea of the location of America relative to Siberia, but once again it proved impossible to reach any real understanding of the area. There were rumours of land just across the water from the Kamchatkan shore. Was this America, or only islands? No one knew. By 1731 preparations were under way for a second Bering expedition.

Without the driving force of Peter the Great, it was hard to get anything done in Russia. Bering fumed impatiently while the Government organized the expedition at a snail's pace. The plans were changed several times. Bering did not get his final instructions until December 1732. He was ordered to explore Kamchatka thoroughly and to send two vessels across the water to the bodies of land in the east. Scientists were to accompany the party to study the mineral wealth of the region, the wild-life, and the native peoples.

Advance groups set out from the Russian city of St Petersburg in February 1733. Bering himself left in April. His destination was the Siberian port of Okhotsk, where he expected to find two ships in readiness for his voyage. After unbelievable delays, Bering got to Okhotsk in 1735 to discover that the ships had never been built. He requested funds from the government to construct them. Messengers went back and forth across the great distances of Russia, and with fantastic slowness the government eventually approved Bering's request.

As a result of all these delays, the ships were not ready for launching until June of 1740. By then the great explorer had been involved in this expedition for nine years, without yet having gone anywhere of note. He was close to sixty, and worn out by his long struggle with the governmental bureaucracy. His strength was gone and his nerves were badly frayed. But he could not withdraw from the enterprise, after having given so many years to it.

Just as the ships were about to sail, the chief surgeon fell ill. Bering needed a quick replacement – someone who could practise medicine and who could also take a part in the scientific research that was planned. When he learned that a German professor named Georg Wilhelm Steller was in Siberia with the intention of joining the expedition, Bering sent for him at once.

Steller was a brilliant, energetic man full of high ambitions. He had studied medicine, botany, and the natural sciences in his homeland. When through a political mishap he failed to get the professorship he sought in a German university, he took the first job that presented itself: surgeon to a regiment of Russian soldiers heading home from the wars. That was how in 1734, at the age of twenty-five, Steller found himself a citizen of St Petersburg.

He could not speak a word of Russian when he arrived, but he was a quick learner. Soon he held the high post of physician to the Archbishop of Novgorod. But Steller sought some more adventurous outlet for his talents. Learning that Bering, four thousand miles away on the other side of Russia, was preparing for his second expedition, Steller sought an appointment as a botanist on the voyage. In the summer of 1737, the government approved his application and he set out for Kamchatka.

He had married the attractive widow of another explorer, and proposed to take her with him to Siberia. Her first husband had told her, though, what Siberian winters were like. When the Stellers had come only as far east as Moscow, the lady announced that she would go no farther. Steller was forced to choose between his bride and his scientific career. He sent his wife back to St Petersburg, and continued on to Siberia, lonely and embittered.

Bering still knew nothing of Steller's existence. The young German made his way slowly through Siberia – everything seems to have been done terribly slowly in those days – and paused en route to study the wildlife of the snowbound Siberian forests. The fascinations of the wilderness eased the pain of parting from his wife. He was able to write to a friend, 'I have entirely forgotten her and have fallen in love with nature.'

In October 1740 Steller arrived at the Siberian town of Bolsheretsk. Bering learned of his presence and summoned him to Kamchatka the following March. The old, weary Danish explorer interviewed the youthful, self-confident German scientist and signed him on as the ex-

pedition's doctor. After a decade's delay, Bering's two
ships finally sailed from the Kamchatkan port of Petropavlosk on 4 June 1741. Among the seventy-eight
men of the flagship the *St Peter*, was George Wilhelm
Steller.

The voyage started well. With sails high they headed
east-south-east into the Pacific. Somewhere in the fog-
bound sea lay the western coast of America, but no one
knew exactly where. On 20 June, the *St Peter* was
separated in a storm from her companion vessel, the *St
Paul*. Bering's flagship continued safely eastward for six
weeks, running parallel to the island chain known as the
Aleutians. On 16 July the snowy peaks of the Alaskan
mainland came into view.

Steller was delighted. A whole new unexplored land
lay before him, full of unknown plants and animals.
When Bering sent a few crewmen ashore to collect a
supply of fresh water, Steller impulsively leaped into the
boat. Thus he was among the first Europeans to set foot
on Alaskan soil. Hurrying inland, Steller began to gather
specimens of every unfamiliar living thing he saw. He
picked strange plants, observed a previously undis-
covered species of bluejay, and spotted a distant Indian
camp fire.

At four that afternoon Steller returned to the beach.
He loaded his botanical specimens into the boat that was
going back to the *St Peter*, and sent a note to Bering
asking for gifts that he could take to the Indian village.
While he waited for Bering's reply, Steller passed the
time by writing a hasty account of all he had discovered
that day. It took him an hour to list all the new species.
Then came Bering's reply. There would be no visit to
the Indians, said the commander. There would be no
further explorations. The *St Peter* was going to leave

immediately on its return journey, and if Steller did not care to come aboard, he would be left behind.

Steller was outraged at this turn of events. He had envisioned a leisurely exploration of the new land. But Bering, an old and tired man, had lost his stomach for discovery. He had done what the government had asked him to do: he had crossed the strait east of Siberia and had found the western shores of America. Now he was impatient to return.

Unhappy Steller had to yield, and he was whisked away from Alaska after his one day of observations. The *St Peter* started back for Siberia, sailing through the Aleutian Islands. Steller found these northern waters well populated by marine mammals – fur seals, sea lions, porpoises, sea otters, and many other types, which he studied in detail.

The short Arctic summer waned, and the storms of winter descended. Buffeted by icy seas, the *St Peter* made slow progress, and in September many of the sailors were laid low by the plague of seamen, scurvy. Too many months without fruit, vegetables, or fresh meat brought on an epidemic of this disease. The weakened crewmen were harried by gales and high winds, which drove the ship off course. Bering veered north towards the Shumagin Islands in October. Steller went ashore again on one of these islands to help search for edible plants, and had a brief visit with some native Alaskans. But the water collected there proved to be polluted, and many of the men died.

On 4 November 1741 a high body of land loomed out of the stormy sea. The men rejoiced, thinking it was Siberia; they quickly discovered that it was not the mainland at all, but only a large island. They were still hundreds of miles from Kamchatka. The following day Bering and his officers held an urgent meeting. Twelve men already had died, thirty-four were totally disabled by disease, and the rest were weakening fast. Only about ten men were fit for active duty at all. The supply of fresh water was running low the weather grew fiercer every day. They decided it was impossible to get back to the mainland under such conditions. They would spend the winter on this island and try to reach Siberia in the spring.

As the *St Peter* approached a rock-fringed harbour on the island, rough waves seized it and threatened to hurl it to destruction. An anchor was dropped, but the cable snapped. The ship sped in darkness towards certain doom. Then came a miracle: a great wave sent the ship coasting safely over the jagged reef into a quiet bay.

The able-bodied men went ashore, making the first landing on what is now called Bering Island, and began to build huts and dugout shelters along the beach. The sick men were taken from their cabins and brought ashore. Many of them, unable to withstand the shock of fresh air, died as they reached the island. Wild foxes snapped at the corpses, and the survivors strained their endurance to bury their comrades before they were devoured. It took several weeks to get everyone to shore. Bering himself, dejected and ill, was carried to the island on 9 November. He remained gloomily in his hut, scarcely speaking to anyone.

On 28 November a gale blew the anchored *St Peter* on to the beach and wrecked it. This seemed to destroy any hope of ever returning to Siberia, and after the disaster Bering sank into a decline of spirits that ended with his death on 8 December. The survivors now were under the command of two lieutenants, Waxel and Khitrov. But they, too, were sick. The only really healthy man was Dr

Steller. He assumed the leadership of the castaways and ministered to their health.

The island was uninhabited by man, but it was rich in animal life. Large flocks of sea birds nested there. Seals were abundant on the cliffs and rocks, and a variety of large marine mammals inhabited the coastal waters. The men hunted sea otters, flipper-limbed animals with coats of elegant fur. The flesh of the sea otter was tough and leathery, but it proved nourishing. When two whales were stranded on the beach, the explorers slew them and feasted on their blubber. By January fresh meat and fresh water had restored the health of the castaways. No longer required to toil day and night as a physician, Steller now had time for natural history.

As though set loose in paradise, he happily studied the habits of the unfamiliar creatures of the island. The sea otter, because it was so common, received much of his attention. He built a hut on the beach where sea otters came ashore, and spent days hidden in it, observing them. Steller also discovered a large fishing bird that he named the spectacled cormorant. In midwinter, when the sea otters had become scarce, the men turned to these birds for food. A single cormorant weighed twelve to fourteen pounds, and made a meal for three men. It was a handsome bird, with dark green feathers tinged with blue on the neck and purple on the shoulders. Its eyes were ringed with a zone of bare white skin that looked like a pair of spectacles. Though it could fly after a fashion, the spectacled cormorant was slow-moving and of an unsuspicious nature, and it was easy to kill.

As the weather warmed, large herds of new marine mammals came ashore – sea bears, seals, and sea lions. With sea otters now mostly out to sea for the spring, the castaways hunted these animals instead. The meat of seals and sea lions, though, did not seem very tasty. On 21 May 1742, the men made their first attempt to hunt the most remarkable of all the animals of Bering Island: the sea cow.

They had observed this gigantic beast in awe and wonder since their first days on the island. In his account of the wildlife of Bering Island, Steller wrote that sea cows were found 'at all seasons of the year in great numbers and in herds' along the shore, 'especially where streams flow into the sea and all kinds of seaweed are most abundant'.

Sea Cow

Steller's description of the sea cow is worth quoting in detail, because he was the only trained scientist ever to see this mammal alive. The sea cow, he wrote, is '28 to 35 feet long and 22 feet thick about the region of the navel, where they are thickest. To the navel this animal resembles the seal species; from there on to the tail, a fish ... In the mouth it has on each side in place of teeth two wide, longish, flat, loose bones, of which one is fastened above to the palate, the other to the inside of the lower jaw. Both are provided with many obliquely converging furrows and raised welts with which the animal grinds up the seaweeds, its usual food.

'The lips are provided with many strong bristles, of which those on the lower jaw are so thick that they resemble quills of fowls ... The eyes of this animal in spite of its size are not larger than sheeps' eyes [and are] without eyelids. The ears are so small and hidden that they cannot at all be found and recognized among the many grooves and wrinkles of the skin ...

'These animals, like cattle, live in herds at sea, males and females going together and driving the young before them about the shore. They are occupied with nothing else but their food. The back and half the body are always seen out of the water. They eat in the same manner as the land animals, with a slow forward movement. They tear the seaweed from the rocks with their feet and chew it without cessation ... During the eating they move the head and neck like an ox, and after the lapse of a few minutes they lift the head out of the water and draw fresh air with a rasping and snorting sound after the manner of horses. When the tide falls they go away from the land to sea but with the rising tide go back again to the shore, often so near that we could strike and reach them with poles from shore. They are not afraid of man in the least ...'

What Steller had discovered, actually, was the mermaid seen by Henry Hudson's men. There is no other likely explanation. The sea cow was a giant manatee of the Arctic, and Hudson must have come upon one that had wandered far east of its usual habitat. A female sea cow, seen at a great distance, might just have seemed like a mermaid to the sailors.

The sea cows were vast floating meat supplies, but the Russians did not try to hunt them until they had exhausted most of the other available food in their part of the island. Lieutenant Khitrov noted in his logbook that the flesh of the fur seal was 'quite distasteful, and the longer we ate it the less we liked it. We then turned to hunting the sea-cow.'

Steller's journal describes how, on 21 May, they tried to land a sea cow by embedding a large iron hook in its hide and hauling it ashore on a long rope. But the hook was too dull, and the black wrinkled hide of the beast, an inch thick and very much like a layer of cork, was too tough and firm. In June, after repairing the ship's yawl, several of the sailors went out in the boat to harpoon a sea cow. Steller wrote: 'A harpooner with a steersman and four oarsmen were put in the yawl, and a harpoon given the first together with a very long line, coiled in proper order as in whaling, its other end being held on shore by the other forty men. We now rowed very quietly towards the animals, which were browsing in herds along the shore in the greatest security. As soon as the harpooner had struck one of them the men on the shore gradually pulled it towards the beach; the men in the yawl rushed upon it and by their commotion tired it out further; when it seemed enfeebled they jabbed large knives and bayonets into its body until it had lost almost all its blood which spurted from the wounds as from a fountain, and could thus be hauled on the beach at high tide and made fast. As soon as the water went out again and the animal lay on the dry beach the meat and fat were cut off everywhere in pieces and carried with rejoicing to our dwellings, where the meat was kept in barrels and the fat hung up on high frames.'

Steller told a touching story of the loyalty of these enormous creatures: 'When one of them was hooked, all the others were intent upon saving him. Some tried to prevent the wounded comrade from being drawn on the beach by forming a closed circle around him; some attempted to upset the yawl; others laid themselves over the rope or tried to pull the harpoon out of his body, in which indeed they succeeded several times. We also noticed, not without astonishment, that a male came two days in succession to its female which was lying dead on the beach, as if he would inform himself about her condition. Nevertheless, no matter how many of them were wounded and killed, they always remained in one place.'

The meat, Steller reported, was excellent. Each sea cow provided more than seven thousand pounds of meat and fat. The deep red flesh tasted much like good beef. 'All of us who had partaken of it,' Steller said, 'soon found out what a salutary food it was, as we soon felt a marked improvement in strength and health.' They boiled the fat, which had the look and consistency of olive oil, and drank it by the cupful in great pleasure.

It was now June, and time to be thinking of the homeward journey. The shipwrecked mariners, greatly improved in health and morale by their winter's stay on the island, demolished the shattered *St Peter* and assembled a new craft from the old timbers. By August 1742 they were ready to set out. They provisioned their vessel with sea-cow meat, enough to last them for a lengthy voyage, and sailed westward for the mainland. On 25 August they sighted Kamchatka, and anchored two days later at Petropavlosk. Thirty-two men, including the commander, had died on the voyage.

But Alaska had been discovered, and Steller had brought back with him a wealth of scientific information. Few naturalists had ever come upon so many new species in so short a time. He settled in Kamchatka and continued his research, mounting his specimens and writing lengthy accounts of the sea cow and the other newly found creatures.

He had always been a man with a sharp tongue, though, who spoke out freely when he pleased. While in Kamchatka, Steller said something that offended the local governor, and he was arrested and taken to an inland city for trial. Found innocent and released, he gained permission to return to St Petersburg to make an official report on his exploits. When he was half-way home, he was arrested again and ordered back to Siberia for a new trial. Then, on the eastward trek, word came that he did not need to stand trial after all. He was worn out by this constant back-and-forth travel over the frozen wastes, and his fatigued body was unable to withstand a sudden fever that struck him in November 1746. Within a few days he was dead, at the age of thirty-seven.

Steller was buried in a shallow grave on the banks of a Siberian river. Not long afterwards the river flooded and carried away his bones. No one even knows what he looked like, for he never posed for a portrait. Though his remains were lost, Steller's research is his monument. He managed to write before he died a book called *De Bestis Marinis*, 'On Marine Animals', and when it was published in 1751 it established him as one of the great naturalists of his time. The sea cow that he discovered was given the scientific name of *Rhytina stelleri*, 'Steller's wrinkled one'. His name has also been given to a blue-jay, a duck, a mollusc, three types of fishes, a sea lion, several species of plants, and two mountains, so he does not lack for recognition.

Of all Steller's discoveries, the sea cow was the strangest and also the most tragic. This harmless, inoffensive animal, which wanted only to be left alone to

77

browse on seaweed in its chilly coastal home, was quickly hunted into extinction.

The sea cow was rare to begin with. It belonged to the family of sirenians, and was related to those false mermaids of the tropics, the dugong and the manatee. Somehow it had adapted itself to Arctic life, growing to colossal size and settling in just one place – the lonely islands of the Bering Sea, between Alaska and Siberia. A scientist who studied this region in the nineteenth century estimated that there had been no more than fifteen hundred sea cows when the *St Peter* reached Bering Island in 1741. The gigantic size of the sea cows may be a clue that the species was nearing natural extinction, for giantism is often one of the last stages in the life span of a species. From Steller's evidence, it seems that the birth rate of the sea cows was low, another sign of an exhausted stock.

Scarcity, low birth rate, harmlessness – these factors made the sea cow a likely victim of extinction. Its meat was tasty. It had no way of defending itself. It was too ponderous to escape from an attack.

Steller and his stranded companions were only indirectly responsible for the disappearance of the sea cow. They did not kill any of the animals until six weeks before their departure from Bering Island, and it seems that they killed only two all told – forgivable enough, considering that they were shipwrecked men in need of food. But when the voyagers returned to Kamchatka, they brought along the handsome pelts of sea otters. The Russians, who had been the world's leading fur traders for centuries, instantly saw a source of rich profits in this newly discovered animal. Within a few years, Russian ships were wandering up and down the Bering Sea in search of sea otters.

The perfect port of call for these expeditions was Bering Island. Nearly every ship stopped there to stock up with provisions. It was the only place where sea cows could be found, and the sea cow was ideal food for the sea-otter hunters. Skilled harpooners found it child's play to kill a sea cow; and when one animal was attacked, its companions, instead of fleeing, flocked around it and exposed themselves to the harpoons as well. Sometimes a wounded sea cow sank to the bottom before it could be butchered, but that was no loss; there were dozens more near at hand to be slaughtered.

A book about the Russian fur trade published in 1776 lists some of the visits to Bering Island after Steller. There are four entries:

'Ivan Krassilnikov's vessel started first in 1754 and arrived on 8th October at Bering Island, where all the vessels fitted out for hunting the sea-otter on the remote islands are wont to pass the winter, in order to provide themselves with a sufficient stock of the flesh of the sea cow.'

'The autumn storms, or rather the wish to take on board a stock of provisions, compelled a number of hunters sent out by the merchant Tolstyk to touch at Bering Island, where, during the winter up to 13th June, 1757, they obtained nothing else than sea cows, sea lions, and large seals. They found no sea-otters this year.'

'A hunting vessel under Commander Studenzov landed on Bering Island in 1758 to kill sea cows, as all vessels are accustomed to do.'

'After Korovin in 1762 on Bering Island had provided himself with a sufficient stock of the flesh and hides of the sea cow for his boats . . . he sailed on.'

It was easy butchery. The harpoons flashed, and the bulky, helpless sea cows died. The tender meat of the mountainous beasts was too tempting to pass by, and the sea cows, unlike the sea otters and seals, lacked the intelligence to go into hiding when the Russian boats appeared. Another victim was the spectacled cormorant, that plump, glossy green bird discovered by Steller. It, too, had delicious meat and was slow to take flight. The hunters killed it cheerfully, until one day no one knowns exactly when – there were no spectacled cormorants left anywhere.

As early as 1755, a Russian geologist named Jakovlev, who visited the islands of the Bering Sea looking for copper mines, realized that the sea cow was doomed. He petitioned the authorities at Kamchatka to put the animal under protection of law before it was exterminated. Nothing was done, however.

The last time any of the Russian fur hunters recorded killing a sea cow on Bering Island was 1768. Four years later, a ship commanded by one Dmitri Bragin spent the winter there. Captain Bragin, at the request of a Russian zoologist, kept a journal in which he listed all the large marine animals he saw on the island. The sea cow was not mentioned.

Another hunting expedition passed the winter of 1783–1784 on Bering Island. No sea cows were seen.

The sea otters, too, suffered from the hunting. They were killed by the thousands and the tens of thousands until so few remained that it was no longer profitable to go after them. Probably that fact is all that spared the sea otter from extinction. The sea-otter trade dropped to next to nothing during the early nineteenth century. When the United States bought Alaska from Russia in 1867, the slaughter began again, and in 1873 more than four thousand were killed, possibly half of all those that still remained. The government finally took action to discourage the hunting of the sea otter, but it was not until 1910 that an international treaty prohibited killing it. Today about ten thousand sea otters live along the Alaskan and Aleutian coasts.

For the sea cow the outcome was less happy. It was too slow and too few in numbers to survive more than thirty years of hunting by man. So far as anyone knows officially, the sea cow became extinct in 1768. Skeletons were collected by many European museums, which proudly displayed mounted specimens more than thirty feet long. Steller's account of the sea cows became a priceless document, for it contained all the information anyone had about the living animals.

For a long while the sea cow was regarded as a type of whale. But it was clear from Steller's description that it was a huge sirenian. Its physical shape and its habits linked it to the dugongs and the manatees, while its two large breasts qualified it as a 'mermaid'.

The discovery of a fossil animal in Egypt shed some light on the ancestry of the sirenians, early in the nineteenth century. An animal known as a *Moeritherium* was found, about the size of a pig, with a stocky body and a broad, fleshy upper lip. It seemed to bear a relation both to certain fossil sirenian forms and to fossil elephants. It is thought that the *Moeritherium* represents an early form of a family that took two evolutionary directions. One branch, accustomed to grazing in swamps and marshes, eventually became aquatic, its limbs evolving into flippers. These were the sirenians. The other branch, remaining on land, developed a long trunk and tusks. These were the elephants. Although at a glance it does not appear that the sea cow and the elephant have much more in common than their great size, evidently they share a common ancestry.

Late in the nineteenth century, a Swedish naturalist named A. E. Nordenskiöld made an important voyage of scientific discovery in the Arctic aboard his yacht, the *Vega*. When he reached the islands of the Bering Sea, he asked the natives about sea cows, in the remote hope that they could lead him to a live one. Nordenskiöld did not see any sea cows, but he did hear a couple of stories that led him to think that at least a few had survived past 1768.

An elderly man, the son of a Russian and an Aleutian woman, reported that his father had left Russia to settle on Bering Island at the age of seventeen, in 1777. 'The two or three first years of his stay there,' Nordenskiöld was told, 'sea cows were still being killed as they pastured on seaweed. The heart only was eaten and the hide used for making boats ... After that time no sea cows were killed.'

Nordenskiöld also was informed by two other men that about 1855 'on the east side of the island they had seen an animal unknown to them which was very thick before, but grew smaller behind, had small fore-feet, and appeared with a length of about fifteen feet above water, now raising itself up, now lowering itself. The animal "blew", not through blowholes, but through the mouth, which was somewhat drawn out. It was brown in colour with some lighter spots.'

Nordenskiöld questioned the two men thoroughly and concluded to his own satisfaction that 'the animal which they saw was actually a sea cow', since their description almost exactly matched Steller's account in a number of important respects, and they could not possibly have seen that account.

Although unable to find a live sea cow, Nordenskiöld had considerable success in obtaining the bones of one.

The natives had made a habit of digging up sea cow bones in a grassy bank near a stream, where they were found in great abundance, and using the huge ribs as runners for their sleds. When Nordenskiöld offered to pay for sea cow remains, 'a great part of the male population now began to search for bones very eagerly, and in this way I collected such a quantity that twenty-one casks, large boxes, or barrels were filled with *Rhytina* bones; among which were three fine, complete skulls, and others more or less damaged, several considerable collections of bones from the same skeleton, etc.'

Did Steller's sea cow really survive the onslaught of the Russian hunters?

A. E. Nordenskiöld thought so. But he had nothing more to go by than the stories of possibly unreliable old men.

For eighty years nothing more was heard of the sea cow. Then, in the August 1963 issue of the Russian magazine *Priroda*, 'Nature', the official journal of the Academy of Science of the U.S.S.R., came a new report.

In the summer of 1962, the article declared, the captain and crew of the Russian whaling ship *Buran* saw a group of large marine mammals in shallow water off a cape north-east of Kamchatka. They were twenty to twenty-four feet long and were grazing in a dense pasture of seaweed. The animals were not whales or seals. They were dark in colour, with large upper lips. No specimens were taken.

What did the Russians see?

Quite possibly it was the world's last herd of sea cows, which had quietly gone on living off the Siberian coast all these years. There are many unexplored places in the Arctic, and there is no reason why a few sea cows could not have slipped away and gone unnoticed since the eighteenth century. Until some solid proof of their existence is forthcoming, though, we must class this bulky mermaid among the animals exterminated by man.

5

The Great Auk

The penguin is a bird of the southern hemisphere. The eighteen species of penguins known today all live south of the equator – two types in Antarctica, others in Australia, New Zealand, South America and Africa. These solemn, dignified-looking flightless birds were not discovered until the sixteenth century, when the first European explorers ventured into the part of the world where they live.

But once there were 'penguins' in the northern hemisphere, too. Though not at all related to the penguins we know, they actually were the first birds to bear that name. The penguins of the south were named after them because of the resemblance they had to these northern birds.

Today the original penguin is extinct. When we come upon references to penguins found in places like Newfoundland and Iceland, we must realize that a bird entirely different from what we know as a penguin is meant.

The penguin of the north is more properly known as the great auk or giant auk. Auks are birds of the northern seas, with heavy bodies, small wings, and broadly webbed feet. They have thick, waterproof plumage and are powerful swimmers. Though the surviving species of auks are able to fly, they prefer to spend their time in the sea, where they feed on small fish and crustaceans. They dive to great depths in search of their food, and are protected against the water pressure by a flat plate of bone and cartilage within the breast and abdomen. There are some two dozen members of the auk family, including such birds as the puffin, the guillemot, the dovekie, the

Great Auk

murre, the auklet, and the razor-billed auk. Most of them are odd-looking birds with curiously prominent beaks. Without exception, they prefer the chilly north, and are most abundant in places like Alaska, Canada, Greenland, and the islands of the Arctic Ocean. They pass much of their time at sea, feeding and sleeping on the water, and only at nesting time do they come ashore to lay their eggs. Their favourite nesting places are on lonely islands and bleak, rocky coasts.

The largest member of the auk family, the great auk, was a bird that stood about two feet high. In colour it looked much like a familiar penguin: black above, white below, as if it were wearing evening clothes. Its head was dark brown and it had a large patch of white on each side of the face, between the eye and the beak. Its big black beak was striped with white grooves.

On land, the great auk was a clumsy sight, taking short waddling steps on its large webbed feet and waving its short flipperlike wings in the air to steady itself. It would stand upright, penguin-fashion. Once it was in the water, it was far more effective. It swam rapidly, using its flippers and broad feet to propel itself, drawing in its neck and lifting its head. It could swim great distances without tiring and could dive to unusual depths. A swimming great auk moved so swiftly that it could not be overtaken by pursuers in rowing boats.

On land, though, it was a different story. The auk was slow and ungainly and could easily be captured. Since its meat was considered a delicacy, and its body was covered with a thick layer of fat that was useful as fuel, the great auk was frequently the target of hunters.

In prehistoric times the great auk had a wide range of habitat. Even though it could not fly, its exceptional abilities as a swimmer took it to many parts of the world. Its main home was the north, from Russia and Scandinavia in the east to Canada in the west. But fossil great auks have been discovered on the coast of Italy and along the Atlantic shoreline of America from Maine to Florida. It is one of the birds depicted in prehistoric cave murals in northern Spain.

The Dodo, the Auk and the Oryx

Ancient man hunted the great auk until it was extinct in those parts of the world where it could easily be found. Heaps of auk bones have been excavated at the sites of Indian camping grounds in New England. Vast deposits of them have been unearthed in the refuse dumps of Scandinavian villages of five thousand years ago. Like the dodo, like the sea cow, the great auk was too easy to kill. It did not stand a chance.

Eventually it was gone from all the settled countries, and probably was forgotten for centuries. Most likely the rediscovery of the great auk by Europeans began about nine hundred years ago, with the voyages of the Viking sea rovers. As these hardy navigators made their way westward from Scandinavia to Iceland, from Iceland to Greenland, from Greenland to the mainland of North America, they must certainly have come upon islands where thousands of large, fat, flightless birds made their nests. In the Norse Eddas, the epic poems of Viking times, the great auk is referred to as the *geirfugl*. Some say that this word became the English word garefowl, as the great auk sometimes was called. Another version has it that the fishermen of Ireland and Scotland, finding the bird on the islands of the North Atlantic, gave it the Gaelic name of *gearrabhul*, 'the strong stout bird with the spot', which later was corrupted to garefowl.

What is certain is that the Vikings hunted the great auk from Iceland to Newfoundland. By A.D. 1000 it was no longer very common on the European side of the Atlantic, but in the west it existed in such multitudes that the raids of the Norsemen had no effect on its numbers. When the Viking voyages ceased, some time in the twelfth or thirteenth century, the great auks of Newfoundland, Labrador, and Greenland were left in peace for several hundred years.

Late in the fifteenth century fishermen from Portugal, Spain, and France began to go boldly westward in quest of codfish. Their boats had to travel well out into the Atlantic to find the cod, which liked the cool waters off Newfoundland. Some of these unknown fishermen may actually have discovered North America a generation before Columbus sailed. Beyond a doubt they discovered the outlying islands on which the great auk nested.

It became customary for the fishing boats to call at these islands and raid the colonies of auks for meat. The birds were attacked with clubs; they protested loudly, squawking in harsh and croaking tones, and sometimes inflicted savage bites on their tormentors, but when caught on land they were too slow to escape. They were clubbed to death by the hundreds and loaded aboard the boats. Some were eaten fresh, the rest were salted down to be used as provisions during the rest of the voyage. The large eggs of the great auk, yellowish-white with black and brown splotches, were collected in huge quantities. Since each great auk laid only one egg a season, taking these eggs was a serious threat to the survival of the species. But so many millions of auks lived on the islands that no one could imagine a time when there would be none.

John Cabot encountered great auks on the Labrador coast in 1497. His son Sebastian reported seeing them in the Hudson Straits twenty years later. An entry in the journal of the French explorer, Jacques Cartier, describes the meeting between man and auk on Funk Island, off Newfoundland, in 1534. Cartier had sent two boatloads of men ashore to gather provisions. They found the island thronging with great auks, so trusting that they let the men approach them. 'In less than half an hour,' Cartier wrote, 'we filled two boats full of them, as if they had been stones. So that besides them which we did eat fresh, every ship did powder and salt five or six barrels of them.'

The slaughter continued all during the sixteenth and seventeenth centuries. Fishermen in northern waters depended on the great auk for their food supplies, and after Newfoundland was colonized the settlers made regular visits to the nesting grounds of the auk to kill the birds and salt them for winter eating. New uses were developed, too. The feathers were sought for feather beds. The meat, when too much was available for men to eat, was used as bait by fishermen. The fat became oil to burn in lamps and on stoves. Many an auk was cooked on a fire fed with auk fat. A dried auk, its body full of oil, made a handy torch. The collarbones of the auk were excellent as fish-hooks. It seemed as though Divine Providence had obligingly granted this bird of so many uses to the colonists of the north. One man wrote in 1622, 'God made the innocencie of so poor a creature to become such an admirable instrument for the sustentation of man.'

It was in the sixteenth century that the great auk already known as a *geirfugl*, a garefowl and a *gearrabhul*, first was termed a penguin. The derivation of the word is obscure. According to one story, the fishermen of Brittany gave the bird a Celtic name, *pen-gwyn*, 'white head'. Some scholars claim, though, that the word is derived from the Latin *pinguis* which means 'fat'. A third school holds that the name comes from the verb 'to pinion', meaning to make a bird unable to fly. The flightless great auk was the 'pinion-winged bird', which became 'pin-wing' and then 'penguin'. Whatever the explanation, the great auk acquired a new name. Later in the sixteenth century, when Sir Francis Drake and other voyagers to high southern latitudes discovered a different black and white flightless bird, it was quite natural for them to term it a 'southern penguin'.

The southern penguin is still with us, but the persecution of the penguin of the north became a campaign of total extermination. Stone corrals were constructed on the auk islands and the birds were driven into them to be killed. The summer – the nesting season – was the only time at which the auks could be taken, for the rest of the year they lived at sea and were safe from human marauders. So each summer the men came and camped and killed. Slaying the auks during the nesting season com-

Great Auk

pounded the slaughter, for each time a female auk was killed it meant one less auk in the next generation as well.

Still, by 1730 millions of auks remained in Greenland, according to the explorer and missionary Hans Egede. In another generation, though, the great auk had become a scarce bird even there. Two hundred and fifty years of uninterrupted butchery had taken their toll. The only places where the great auk survived were rocky islets off

Newfoundland, Greenland, and Iceland, and on the island of St Kilda off the coast of Scotland.

It no longer was practical to launch large-scale auk-hunting expeditions, but free-lance parties of local men still raided the nests of the auk for their tasty eggs. Evidently the eggs must have been a wonderful delicacy, because the remaining auk nests were found on inaccessible, barren islands surrounded by cold, choppy seas, and many of the hunters lost their lives attempting to reach them.

The last great auk on St Kilda was killed in 1821. The Newfoundland auks had already become extinct. The egg collectors had done their work so well that the only place where the great auk still existed was on a group of islands known as the Auk Rocks at the south-western tip of Iceland. The villagers of the district made regular trips to the Auk Rocks to collect eggs and occasionally to kill the birds.

Most of the auks of the Auk Rocks withdrew to a lonely outcropping of rock called Geirfuglasker, 'Geirfugl Island'. Here, it seemed, they were safe from the peasants and fishermen. But nature herself seemed determined to sweep the great auk from the face of the earth. In 1830, a volcano erupted under the sea near Iceland, causing a seaquake that changed the contours of the coast line. Geirfuglasker disappeared beneath the waves. The last home of the great auk was gone.

At this point, the museum directors of the world awoke to the fact that a species that once had numbered in the millions was virtually extinct. The Geirfuglasker catastrophe might well have killed all the great auks that had survived the hunters. What worried the museum directors was that there were hardly any specimens of the great auk in their collections – no skeletons, no stuffed birds, no eggs. John Tradescant, the Englishman who had left a stuffed dodo to Oxford, had also owned a stuffed great auk, and there was another specimen in a Belgian collection. Otherwise there was practically nothing. Frantically, the museums sent out word that they needed great auks.

Now began one of the most bitterly ironic tales of any creature's extinction. It turned out that about fifty great auks had survived the sinking of Geirfuglasker. While the island was going down, these birds had managed to take refuge on a much smaller island nearby, called Eldey.

Did the museum directors immediately see to it that the last fifty auks were rounded up and placed under protection to keep the species alive?

No.

What they wanted was something to go in display cases. They wanted stuffed birds, and were willing to pay good prices for them. Fabulous sums were offered for the complete skin of a great auk or for a skeleton or for an unbroken egg.

To the people of that part of Iceland it was an attractive business deal. It was fairly easy to row over to Eldey, kill a great auk without damaging it unduly, and collect a handsome fee from some eager museum representative. Between 1830 and 1844 one bird after another was hunted down, until just two were left.

On 4 June 1844 three fishermen named Jon Brandsson, Sigurdr Islefsson, and Ketil Ketilsson made a trip to Eldey. They had been hired by an Icelandic bird collector named Carl Siemsen, who wanted auk specimens. Jon Brandsson found an auk and killed it. Sigurdr Islefsson found another and did the same. Ketil Ketilsson had to return empty-handed, because his two companions had just completed the extinction of the great auk.

Mr Siemsen got his birds, had them stuffed, and sold them to museums. Now some fifty stuffed great auks were on exhibition in various museums, but there were none left alive anywhere. Later in the nineteenth century came two reports of great auks seen in Newfoundland, but neither account was verified.

Only once has a species been destroyed in the name of science. The greed and cruelty of the hunters reduced the great auk to a handful of survivors, but it was the foolishness of the museum directors that brought down the final curtain. Each one wanted to have an auk to display, and none paid any heed to the fate of the species.

It turned out that the criminal destruction of the auks of Eldey by the museum men was not only stupid but needless. In 1863 an American businessman began to mine guano – bird droppings used for fertilizer – on Penguin Island, Newfoundland. When an excavation was made, a cache of frozen great auks was found, many of them fully preserved in layers of peat. More than a hundred of these birds were recovered, enough to supply all the museums that had paid fancy prices to have the world's last great auks killed.

Once it was clear that the auk was extinct, collectors began to bid frantically for the available specimens. In Europe, particularly in Great Britain, collecting birds' eggs and stuffed birds was a popular hobby. The rich collectors were willing to pay almost any price for the egg of a great auk, no matter how cracked or dirty it might be. Since only seventy-five eggs and eighty complete and undamaged birds had been preserved, it was an important event whenever an egg or a bird came on the market. At an auction in London in 1934 six eggs were sold at prices ranging from £200 to £600 each, depending on condition. Two mounted birds brought £1,650.

If such an auction were held today, the prices might be ten times as high. But few if any auk eggs or skins are in private hands any more. Nearly all are owned by museums, which would not think of selling them.

The great auk's path to doom followed a familiar pattern. The bird was slow-moving – at least on land – and comparatively helpless. It could not fly. Man found its flesh was edible. It did not reproduce in large quantities. Once the killing began, there were fewer auks each year than the year before, until a population of millions was reduced to a few hundred. An upheaval of nature took care of most of those, and the folly of misguided scientists destroyed the rest. The dodo was wiped out in less than a hundred years, the sea cow in less than thirty; the killing of the great auk took centuries, only because there were so many of them to begin with.

The other penguin, the one that got its name because it happened to look like the great auk, might easily have taken the same journey to oblivion, for, when on land, it is just as helpless and defenceless as its extinct northern namesake. The first explorers who visited the Antarctic and other southern haunts of the penguin did indeed slaughter it just as indiscriminately as the New-foundland colonists slew the auk. When Sir Francis Drake passed through the Strait of Magellan in 1578 on his voyage around the world, his men discovered penguins and killed them enthusiastically. Francis Fletcher, the chaplain of the expedition, wrote that 'we found great store of fowl which could not fly, of the bigness of geese, whereof we killed in less than one day 3,000 and victualled ourselves thoroughly therewith'.

A typical penguin hunt was described this way in 1823 by René Lesson, who took part in an expedition to the southerly Falkland Islands:

'Parties of eight to ten men each were armed with sticks and sent out. They walked softly forward, occupied all the paths, and struck down the birds. Their heads had to be smashed in, so that they could not rise and flee. The penguins screamed heartrendingly and defended themselves with furious pecks. In five to ten hours the men slaughtered on an average sixty to eighty birds.'

Two factors helped the penguins to avoid the fate of the great auk. For one, by all accounts their meat is far from delicious, so they were killed for food only when other provisions were lacking. For another, the great auk's nesting grounds were on islands easily reached from North America and Europe, while most penguins are found in uninhabited, inaccessible places. It was the bad luck of the great auk to taste good and to live within the reach of man.

6

The Quagga

Thomas Pringle, a Scottish poet who lived from 1789 to 1834, will never be ranked with Shakespeare and Milton. Forgotten though he is, Pringle had at least one literary distinction. He lived in South Africa for three years as a government librarian, and in 1828 published a number of poems describing the things he saw there. Thomas Pringle is probably the only man who ever mentioned the quagga in a poem.

In his 'Afar in the Desert' he wrote:

> *Afar in the Desert I love to ride,*
> *With the silent Bush-boy alone by my side:*
> *O'er the brown Karoo where the bleating cry*
> *Of the springbok's fawn sound plaintively*
> *And the timorous quagga's shrill whistling neigh*
> *Is heard by the fountain at twilight grey.*

It is not great poetry, but it provides us with a morsel of fact about the quagga that we might otherwise not know. Thomas Pringle was fortunate enough to hear the quagga's 'shrill whistling neigh', but that neigh will never be heard again. The last quagga in the world died in 1883.

The quagga was a type of zebra; and a zebra is just a horse with a striped coat. Quaggas, zebras, horses, donkeys, jackasses, burros, ponies, and other similar animals are all classed in the genus *Equus*. They are distinguished by their long necks and heads, their strong, nimble legs, and their single-hoofed feet. The true horse, *Equus caballus* is descended from the wild horses of Asia.

The playboy of the family is the African zebra. Zebras were known in Europe as long ago as the second century A.D. The Roman historian Dio Cassius writes of 'the horses of the sun which resemble tigers', an unmistakable reference to the zebra's handsome stripes. There are three subspecies of zebra and about twenty local forms, differing from one another in the arrangements of the stripes. Some of these zebra varieties are nearly extinct, such as the cape mountain zebra of South Africa, of which less than a hundred survive in a national park in Cape Province. Though zebras are fast-moving and sturdy animals, they have long been hunted in Africa for their hides. Since they thrive well in captivity, they are not likely to die out altogether, even if all the remaining wild zebras are killed by hunters.

The quagga can best be described as an unfinished zebra. It had stripes, too, but only on its head, neck, shoulders and part of its trunk. The rest of the body was a light chestnut brown in colour, or sometimes yellowish-red, and the legs were white. The mane was dark brown with pale stripes, and a broad dark line ran down the middle of the back. It was as though nature had begun to give the quagga a zebra's stripes and had abandoned the job when it was half done.

It was never a common animal; it was found only in one part of the world. The quagga's range was on the huge plains of South Africa, from the Cape of Good Hope as far north as the Vaal River. In this enormous expanse of open country the quagga grazed in herds of twenty to forty, little islands of brown against the green of the vegetation. Frequently the quagga herds were accompanied by flocks of ostriches and herds of the white-tailed gnu.

Until the seventeenth century the plains where the quagga roamed were inhabited only by the Hottentots, simple nomad huntsmen. The Portuguese voyagers who were the first Europeans to reach South Africa did not care to settle there, regarding it as lacking in natural resources, and the region was generally ignored until the Dutch planted a colony there in 1652. The Dutch colony at the Cape of Good Hope expanded slowly, clearing out the Hottentots and the even more primitive Bushmen of the deserts. A breed of tough African-born Dutchmen, the Boers, emerged. They established large farms, forcing the natives into slavery. Much of South Africa was too dry for farming, and the Boers raised cattle in the arid lands. It was hard, demanding country that produced a race of tireless, stern, deeply religious men.

As the Boers moved inland from their starting point at the Cape, they encountered and began to hunt the numerous animals of the plains. Herds of antelope, up to fifty thousand strong, raced gracefully across the open country, *veldt*, as the Boers called it; zebras and gnus and gazelles were common. Many of the beasts of the veldt had never been seen by white men before. The Boers gave them Dutch names. The gnu, an animal which looks like an ox but is really related to the antelopes, was called the *wildebeest*. An antelope with oddly ridged horns got the name of *hartebeest*. Another, which the natives called the *sassaby*, the Boers christened the *blesbok*.

One animal that did not get a Dutch name was the quagga. This part-striped zebra was known to the Hottentots as the *quahkah*, a name that imitated the animal's barking neigh. To the Boers, the sound it made sounded more like '*qay-hay*', with the stress on the *hay*, but they adopted a modified form of the Hottentot name and called it the *quagga*. As for the true zebra – the one with stripes all the way down – the Boers spoke of it as the *bonte-quagga*, meaning 'the painted quagga' or 'the quagga with conspicuous stripes.'

The first published reference to the quagga appeared in a book by a man named Tachard, in 1685. He called it a *wilde esel*, 'wild ass', and described it in such an inaccurate way that he obviously had not seen it at first hand. In the middle of the eighteenth century a pair of quaggas was captured and shipped to London. A colour plate of the female was published in a book written in 1758 by George Edwards, a naturalist and the librarian of the Royal College of Physicians. In his *Gleanings of Natural History*, Edwards wrote: 'This curious animal was brought alive, together with the male, from the Cape of Good Hope: the male dying before they arrived at London, I did not see it; but this female lived several years at a house of his Royal Highness the Prince of Wales, at Kew ... The noise it made was much different from that of an ass, resembling more the confused barking of a mastiff-dog. It seemed to be of a savage and fierce nature: no one would venture to approach it, but a gardener in the Prince's service, who was used to feed it and could mount on its back. I saw it eat a large paper of tobacco, paper and all; and I was told, it would eat flesh, or any kind of food they would give it. I suppose that proceeded from necessity, or habit, in its long sea-voyage; for it undoubtedly feeds naturally much as horses and asses do, I mean on vegetables.'

Since Edwards saw only a female quagga, he assumed

– incorrectly – that this animal was simply a female zebra. (Edwards had never seen a real female zebra.) He identified it that way in his book, though the plate leaves no doubt it was a quagga. A few years later, a traveller in South Africa was able to determine that the male of the species had the same colouring as the female, and that the quagga was stockier and stronger than the true zebra.

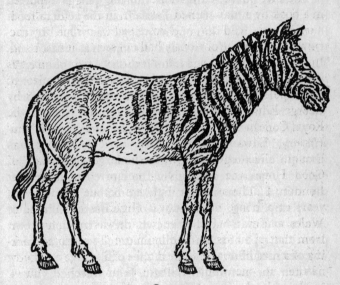

Quagga

The mistaken idea was put to rest for good by a Swedish naturalist named Andrew Sparrman, who explored South Africa in 1775. His book, *A Voyage to the Cape of Good Hope*, published in 1786, provided a detailed account of the quagga that left no doubt that it was distinct from the other zebras. Sparrman had an opportunity to examine at close range a tame quagga that had been caught when young by the Hottentots and kept as a pet. It was prized because it would protect the sheep and horses of the Hottentots against the raids of hyenas and wild dogs.

Horsemeat has never been very popular among Europeans, and the Boers had no desire to hunt quaggas for food for themselves. However, their Hottentot workers liked the taste of quagga, and Boer hunting parties brought back large numbers of the animals from the veldt as food for the slaves. The skin of the quagga was valued by the Boers for making the leather shoes known as *veldschoen*. They also turned quagga hides into sacks for the storage of grain, dried fruits, and dried meat. The continued hunting of the quagga made deep inroads in its numbers. By the beginning of the nineteenth century the quagga was well on the road to extinction. Vast numbers of them still could be seen, but the appearances were deceptive; what no one realized was that the large gatherings of quaggas represented virtually the entire population of the animal. Though seemingly numerous, the quagga was disappearing. Not that any of the Boers would have cared about that, had they known; the destruction of one particular type of zebra hardly mattered so long as there was plenty of other game left in the veldt.

When the naturalist William John Burchell visited South Africa in 1811, he witnessed a quagga hunt, and saw thousands rounded up to be shot: 'I could compare it [the clatter of their hoofs] to nothing but to the din of a tremendous charge of cavalry, or to the rushing of a mighty tempest. I could not estimate the accumulated number at less than fifteen thousand, a great extent of the country being actually chequered black and white with their congregated masses. As the panic caused by the report of our rifles extended, clouds of dust hovered over them, and the long necks of troops of ostriches were also to be seen, towering above the heads of their less gigantic neighbours, and sailing past with astonishing rapidity. Groups of purple sassaybes and brilliant red and yellow hartebeests likewise lent aid to complete the picture, which must have been seen to be properly understood, and which beggars all attempt at description.'

Burchell watched his Hottentot porters feasting on quagga meat. 'Though much praised,' he wrote, 'I felt no desire to make a meal on it.' But on a later trip he was tempted to try it. He declared, 'The novelty, and my own curiosity, must have had some influence on this occasion, since I was induced to consider it good and palatable. It was tender, and possessed a taste which seemed to be between beef and mutton.'

The indiscriminate shooting of the quaggas went on until they began to grow scarce in the vicinity of the Cape Colony. Sir William Cornwallis Harris, discussing the game animals of Africa in a book published in 1840, wrote that the quagga 'was formerly extremely common within the Colony, but vanishing before the strides of civilization, is now to be found in very limited numbers, and on the borders only'. To the north, where the sound of Boer rifles was not yet often heard, the situation was more encouraging. 'On those sultry plains which are completely taken possession of by wild beasts, and may with strict propriety be termed the domains of savage nature, it occurs in interminable herds,' Sir William reported. He wrote lyrically of 'the gay glittering coats of the quagga' sparkling like mica in the sunshine, and described 'long files of quaggas' as they move 'slowly across the profile of the ocean-like horizon, uttering a shrill barking neigh, of which its name forms a correct imitation'. The marching herds reminded him of the procession of a caravan through the desert.

By 1850 the Boers, having massacred most of the wildlife in their own settlement, were going north to raid the herds that had previously been spared. The Hottentots had to be fed, and the flourishing farmers needed more sacks for their grain. The slaughter went on with a mindless persistence for twenty years. Apparently no one stopped to consider that the supply of quaggas was limited and that they were being killed faster than they could breed. Since they were useful, they could have been raised on ranches and killed for their meat and hides at a rate that would have allowed for replacement of the stock, but the concept was too sophisticated for the hunters. As a result they deprived themselves of a valuable beast and deprived the world of an irreplaceable species. The last wild quagga was killed about 1870.

It had been possible to save the European and American bison from extinction by careful breeding of captive stock. Could the same be done for the quagga? Unfortunately, no. The bison herds, at their lowest point, had numbered fifty in Europe and a thousand in America; but by the time the wild quagga became extinct, it was too late to begin a breeding programme in the zoos. Not enough quaggas remained.

At least sixteen live quaggas were shipped to Europe during the eighteenth and nineteenth centuries, beginning with the female George Edwards described in 1758. They were regarded as interesting curiosities, and most of them were imported not by zoos but by wealthy private individuals. An account published in 1827 tells of a pair of quaggas owned by a Mr Parkins that had been tamed and taught to pull a carriage: 'Among the equipages occasionally exhibited in the gay season at Hyde

Park, and other fashionable places of resort, may be seen a curricle drawn by two Couaggas, which seem as subservient to the curb and whip as any well-trained horses.' After these quaggas died, about 1830, their skulls were purchased by a collector, and eventually they reached a London museum.

One of the first zoos to own a quagga was the Jardin des Plantes in Paris. It obtained a sixteen-year-old animal that was notable for its fierce temper when frightened or excited; its keepers soon learned to give it a wide berth when it was in the mood to kick and bite. It died of old age a few years after it arrived.

The London Zoo had three quaggas at various times in the nineteenth century, and at one point even had a mated pair. It purchased a female quagga in 1851, and seven years later obtained a male. There was some hope of saving the species by rearing a herd in captivity, but this pair produced no offspring. The male suffered fatal injuries in 1864 during a fit of rage. The female lived on until 1872. She was the only quagga ever to be photographed alive. When she died, her skeleton was purchased by the Peabody Museum of Natural History at Yale University, where it is kept today.

Two quaggas outlived her – both of them female. One, at the Berlin Zoo, died in 1875. That left only the quagga that had been living in the Amsterdam Zoo since 1867. She expired on 12 August 1883, the last of the quaggas.

It is difficult of course, to say with absolute certainty that any recent animal is totally extinct. The hope still lingers that somewhere, in some unnoticed corners of the world, a few survivors have outlasted the rest of their race. Reports of such survivors generally are heard from time to time for fifty years or so after the death of the last known member of a species. But, alas, they rarely turn out to have any substance.

The quagga has had several posthumous sightings. In 1917 a British officer, Major C. N. Manning, was making an inspection of the Kaoko Veldt of South West Africa, a territory that had recently come under British control. He caught sight of a distant herd of animals of the size and shape of zebras, but brown in colour and striped only on their foreparts. Major Manning had no binoculars, and he was unable to get close enough to the herd for a good look. He reported his find to a local government official, C. M. Hahn, who instituted a search.

No quaggas were found. Hahn finally came to the conclusion that what Manning had seen was a scarce type of zebra known as Hartmann's zebra. He wrote, 'In the hot season, generally at midday, with the sun overhead, Hartmann's zebras from a distance resemble dark brown donkeys. When the heat haze is severe, it is difficult, at times impossible, to discern the dark marking without the aid of binoculars.'

At various times since then, reports have been made of quaggas in the Kaoko Veldt. The most recent of these was in 1940. No one has yet produced a twentieth-century quagga, though, dead or alive.

7

The Moa and
the Rukh

Of all the legendary birds of literature, none is more awesome than the rukh, or roc, of the *Thousand and One
Nights*. That long-suffering sailor, Sinbad, encountered
that mighty bird on his second voyage. He came to a
'beautiful island, abounding with trees bearing ripe
fruits, where flowers diffused their fragrance, with birds
warbling, and pure rivers'. Here Sinbad spied a huge,
puzzling white dome. 'I drew near to it,' he relates, 'and
walked around it, but perceived no door to it; and I
found that I had not strength nor activity to climb it, on
account of its exceeding smoothness. I made a mark at
the place where I stood, and went round the dome
measuring its circumference, and, lo, it was fifty full
paces; and I meditated upon some means of gaining an
entrance to it.'

As Sinbad pondered the dome, he became aware that
the sun had vanished and the sky had grown dark. 'I
therefore imagined,' he tells us, 'that a cloud had come
over it; but this was in the season of summer; so I won-
dered. And I raised my head, and, contemplating that
object attentively, saw that it was a bird, of enormous
size, bulky body, and wide wings, flying in the air; and
this it was that concealed the body of the sun, and veiled
it from view upon the island. At this my wonder

Sinbad and the Rukh

increased, and I remembered a story which travellers and
voyagers had told me long before, that there is in certain
of the islands, a bird of enormous size, called the rukh,
that feedeth its young one with elephants. I was con-
vinced, therefore, that the dome which I had seen was
one of the eggs of the rukh.'

Many other accounts of giant birds emanated from the
region of the Indian Ocean, where Sinbad had had this
adventure. The Greek historian Herodotus learned from
Egyptian priests about a race of huge birds 'beyond the
sources of the Nile' strong enough to carry off men in
their talons. Rabbi Benjamin of Tudela, who travelled
through much of the Near East in the twelfth century
visiting communities of Oriental Jews, heard that when
ships bound for China were in danger of sinking in
stormy seas, the sailors would sew themselves up in hides
and cast themselves into the water, where they would be
seized and carried ashore in the claws of great eagles.
Marco Polo, when he was on his way home from the
court of Kublai Khan in 1294, visited the 'Isle of Magastar' and was told of a bird 'so big in fact that its wings
covered an extent of 30 paces, and its quills were 12 paces
long, and thick in proportion. And it is so strong that it
will seize an elephant in its talons and carry him high
into the air, and drop him so that he is smashed to pieces;
having so killed him the bird swoops down on him and
eats him at leisure.' The name of this bird, Marco
learned, was the rukh.

Marco Polo's 'Magastar' is almost certainly the large
island of Madagascar – the fourth largest in the world –
which lies 250 miles off the eastern coast of Africa. Madagascar is an island of many strange creatures. It has an
earthworm a yard long and an inch thick; it is the home
of a hedgehog-like animal called the tanrek, whose

mouth is larger in proportion to its size than that of any other mammal; on Madagascar is found the aye-aye, a monkey with the grace of a cat and the appearance of something in a dream, with enormous ears and one vastly extended finger for digging insects out of wood. Long ago Madagascar was attached to Africa, but some ancient upheaval separated it, turning it into an isolation ward for a host of odd beasts that became extinct on the mainland. Considering the variety of life on Madagascar, it could very well have been the home of the rukh.

But the largest living bird of Madagascar is the sea eagle, which is little more than two feet long. If the rukh ever dwelt there, it does not do so now. Where did the legend originate?

Arab sailors had visited Madagascar since the early Middle Ages. Many of them had reported tales of the giant bird. One of these tales of an authentic sailor found its way into the *Thousand and One Nights* in Sinbad's story. We know, too, that Marco Polo's journey was real and that Marco was a good observer. So evidently some big bird of Madagascar was the inspiration for the rukh – some bird that had been in existence in the twelfth and thirteenth centuries, but which is extinct now.

When France took possession of Madagascar in 1642, the first governor of the island was a man named Étienne de Flacourt, who showed a deep interest in the natural history of the place. Flacourt published his *History of the Great Island of Madagascar* in 1658. Among the many mysterious creatures he mentioned was the vouron-patra, which he said was 'a giant bird that lays eggs as big as those of an ostrich. It rarely lives in one district, for it is shy and timid and prefers dark places for its habitat. The people keep water in the eggs of the vouron-patra.'

Flacourt was killed by Algerian pirates on his way home to France soon afterwards, and for nearly two hundred years no one gave much thought to the vouron-patra. But in 1832 a French artillery officer in Madagascar, Victor Sganzin, found one native family using as a water bowl a broken eggshell a foot in diameter. The natives told him that such eggs were quite common in certain parts of the island. Sganzin bought the egg and sent it to Jules Verreaux, a French dealer and collector of natural curiosities, who was then in Capetown, South Africa, on a purchasing trip. Verreaux was awed by the egg. He took it with him when he started back to Paris, but the ship he was on was lost at sea, and Verreaux, his newly collected African specimens, and the rukh's egg all went to the bottom.

John Joliffe, the surgeon of a British ship that stopped at Madagascar in 1848, produced the next report. Joliffe became friendly with one M. Dumarele, a merchant from Réunion, who had made several trading voyages to the Madagascar coasts. Joliffe wrote that Dumarele claimed to have seen 'at Port Leven, on the north-west of the island, the shell of an enormous egg, the production of an unknown bird inhabiting the wilds of the country, which held the almost incredible quantity of thirteen *quart wine bottles of fluid!!!*, he having himself carefully measured the quantity ... M. Dumarele offered to purchase the egg from the natives, but they declined selling it, stating that it belonged to their chief, and that they could not dispose of it without his permission. The natives said that the egg was found in the jungle, and observed that such eggs were *very very rarely* met with, and that the bird which produces them is still more rarely seen'.

Joliffe was sceptical but not overly so. He turned his

story over to Hugh Strickland, the expert on dodos, and remarked, 'The sight of one sound egg would be worth a thousand theories.' Strickland agreed. He knew of Flacourt's old report on the vouron-patra, as well as the rukh fables of Sinbad and Marco Polo, and he considered it quite possible that some large ostrich-like bird might lurk in the unexplored jungles of Madagascar.

At last, in 1850, a French merchant captain named Abadie obtained three eggs and some bones and shipped them safely to Paris, where they were studied in awe by Geoffroy Saint-Hilaire, the director of the Paris zoo. Saint-Hilaire reported that the two largest eggs were $13\frac{5}{8}$ inches by $8\frac{1}{2}$ inches and $12\frac{5}{8}$ inches by $15\frac{5}{8}$ inches, the biggest bird eggs ever seen. Each held more than two gallons of fluid. The eggs were capable of holding as much as six ostrich eggs or 150 hen's eggs – enough to make an omelet for 75 people.

On the basis of the eggs and fragmentary bones, Saint-Hilaire pictured a bird something like an ostrich, powerful and flightless, that stood sixteen feet high. He called it *Aepyornis maximus* 'the tallest of the high birds'.

Not until 1866 did a complete *Aepyornis* skeleton come to light in Madagascar. Then it was seen that Saint-Hilaire had let the size of the eggs unduly influence his estimate of the bird's height. Instead of being as tall as a two-storey house, *Aepyornis* had merely been nine or ten feet high. It had weighed nearly half a ton in life, though, so it was hardly inconspicuous.

The mystery of the rukh had been settled to general satisfaction. Obviously this monstrous long-legged bird of the vast eggs, glimpsed in the jungles of Madagascar, had inspired the legends. Of course, *Aepyornis* was unable to fly, and so it could hardly have carried off

Aepyornis maximus

elephants in its talons, nor was it large enough to blot out the sun by spreading its wings. But these were the pardonable exaggerations of story-tellers, and the real rukh was impressive enough.

If it had still existed in Marco Polo's time, the next logical question was: did the *Aepyornis* yet survive in some part of Madagascar?

The natives said it did, but their reports were unreliable. The bones that had been found were in sub-fossil condition – that is, they were only a few hundred years old, and had not yet undergone the changes of true fossilization. The numerous *Aepyornis* eggs discovered later in the nineteenth century also seemed relatively fresh. But none of the explorers found a live *Aepyornis*, and no one to this day has found one. By all indications the big bird died out some 250 years ago, not long after Flacourt's time.

Why did it become extinct? Apparently man was not responsible this time. The natives of Madagascar had no tradition of hunting the vouron-patra for its meat. Though they did gather its eggs, that in itself could not have been enough to destroy the species.

Scientists have suggested that the *Aepyornis* was a resident of jungle swamps. Several hundred years ago the climate of Madagascar changed, becoming much less rainy, and many of the swamps dried up. This drove the *Aepyornis* into an ever narrower habitat, until it could not gather enough food or find the right shelter to survive. Many *Aepyornis* skeletons have been discovered in the dried mud of former swamps, confirming the notion that the last members of the species huddled together there until death overtook them. When Arab and Malay settlers came to Madagascar about a thousand years ago, they began to cut down the virgin forest, and that may have deprived the big birds of their nesting grounds, indirectly contributing to the extinction. Though a few of the birds may have lived on until the eighteenth or nineteenth century, it seems certain that future Sinbads landing on Madagascar are in little danger of encountering the rukh.

Even before the mysterious rukh of Madagascar was shown to be the extinct *Aepyornis*, a related tribe of giant birds had been discovered thousands of miles away in New Zealand. Although these New Zealand giants had never figured in literature, they could well have been the models for the rukh, because some of them were taller even than *Aepyornis*.

New Zealand, like Madagascar, is a living museum of natural wonders. Its two main islands (called North Island and South Island) once were linked to the mainland of Asia through a chain of land bridges running from island to island across the Pacific. But the bridges collapsed ages ago, leaving New Zealand cut off from the rest of the world.

Three-quarters of New Zealand's plants live nowhere else on earth. Such living fossils as the tuatara, a lizardlike reptile more ancient than the dinosaurs, survive there. The birds of New Zealand are flightless forms, such as the odd, comical little kiwi, a sort of midget ostrich no bigger than a hen. The secret of New Zealand's strangeness is the total absence of any beasts of prey. Until man came, bringing with him his dogs and cats, all forms of wildlife were safe from predators. Birds who have no enemies tend to lose the use of their wings. The dodo was one such bird that forgot how to fly; the *Aepyornis* was another; the great auk, another. New Zealand has a parrot that not only does not fly, but makes its home in underground burrows like a rabbit. Flightless cranes, flightless hens, flightless birds of all kinds – New Zealand abounds in them. Unfortunately, birds that have lost the use of their wings cannot suddenly learn to fly again when enemies appear. When man arrived, accompanied by his animals, the flightless birds of New Zealand were easy victims.

The first men to reach New Zealand were Polynesian islanders who came there by canoe more than a thousand years ago. Probably the earliest of these discoverers came there involuntarily, driven by storms or powerful ocean currents. But about A.D. 1300 there was a large-scale migration to New Zealand from the islands of eastern Polynesia. These people were the Maoris, who still maintain the tradition of the Great Fleet that brought them to their new homeland more than six hundred years ago.

The Maoris found handsome, fertile islands that offered an unusual range of climates, from tropical rain forests at one extreme to glacier-covered mountains at the other. They found a land populated by strange birds and reptiles. But there were no mammals at all, except for two species of bats. The dogs that the Maoris brought as pets, the pigs that they raised as livestock, and the rats that came as uninvited stowaways in the big canoes were the first to set foot there. They began at once to prey on the helpless, harmless creatures of New Zealand, attacking the slow-moving flightless birds and raiding their nests for eggs. Some species were wiped out within a few years by the combined onslaught of these new animals and the Maori hunters. Others became scarce to the point of invisibility.

The European discovery of New Zealand came in 1642, when the Dutch explorer, Abel Tasman, saw its mountains from the sea. Tasman named his discovery after a place in his homeland, but did not go ashore. Captain James Cook was the first European to land there, on his memorable exploratory voyage of 1769, and soon afterwards white settlers were arriving. The Maoris were forced to make room.

European scientists were delighted with the unfamiliar plants and animals of New Zealand, and any traveller who returned from that far-off land was sure of a ready audience for the story of his experiences there. Some of the early visitors to New Zealand, about 1800, heard tales from the Maoris of giant birds on South Island. The first man to get some definite evidence was a merchant named Joel S. Polack, who traded in New Zealand between 1834 and 1837. In 1838 Polack published a two-volume book about New Zealand in which he said that he had seen fossil bones of a large ostrich-like bird. The Maoris told him that 'in times long past ... very large birds had existed, but the scarcity of animal food, as well as the easy method of entrapping them, has caused their extermination'. Polack added, though, that among the older Maoris there were traditions of supernatural beings 'in the form of birds, having waylaid native travellers, among the forest wilds, vanquishing them with an overpowering strength, killing and devouring, etc. The traditions are reported with an air of belief that carries conviction'.

About the same time that Polack was discussing big birds with the Maoris, two other men were carrying on a parallel investigation. The Reverend William Williams, a Protestant missionary in New Zealand, had spent most of 1837 translating the New Testament into Maori, and rewarded himself at Christmas time with a holiday in the East Cape district on North Island. He took with him his friend William Colenso, a printer by trade and a naturalist by avocation. They travelled together for many months, and in the summer of 1838 were at the town of Waiapu, about twenty miles from the East Cape. There, Colenso wrote in the *Tasmanian Journal of Natural Science* shortly afterwards, 'I heard from the natives of a certain monstrous animal; while some said it was a bird, and others "a person", all agreed that it was called a *Moa*; – that in general appearance it somewhat resembled an immense domestic cock, with the difference, however, of its having a "face like a man".' Colenso quoted several Maori legends about the moa, such as that 'if any one ventured to approach the dwelling of this wonderful creature, he would be invariably trampled on and killed by it'. Nowhere in Colenso's first report, however, does he indicate that he took these stories seriously.

In 1839 a traveller named John Rule obtained the battered thigh-bone of some huge creature in New Zealand and brought it with him to England to present to Richard Owen, the leading authority on ancient animals. The bone was broken off at both ends and looked badly weather-beaten. At first glance, the famous Professor Owen thought it was a soup bone and that Rule was playing a trick on him. But Rule persuaded him to study it more carefully. Owen compared it with animal skeletons in the British Museum. He thought it might be the thigh-bone of an ox or a horse, but it did not have the right shape; at length he held it next to the skeleton of an ostrich and realized its true identity. In November 1839 Owen told the Zoological Society of London about the bone. It was dangerous, he said, to speculate on the appearance of a creature when there was nothing more to go by than a fragmentary bone; but he was willing to risk his reputation on the statement that there once had existed in New Zealand a flightless bird 'nearly, if not quite, equal in size to the ostrich'.

That gave the moa its first official scientific recognition. Some of Owen's colleagues said it was rash to jump to such a conclusion, but Owen no longer doubted his judgement. He had 500 extra copies of his report printed and shipped to New Zealand to inspire a search for more evidence.

Even before Owen's report reached New Zealand, a box of moa bones arrived in London. They had been collected early in 1839 by the Reverend William Williams and a fellow missionary, the Reverend Richard Taylor. The bones were held up by British customs inspectors, who did not think they ought to be allowed into England, but eventually science triumphed over bureaucracy and the moa relics found their way to Owen for study.

These various discoveries of moa bones inflamed William Colenso, the printer-naturalist who had accompanied the Reverend Mr Williams in 1838. Suddenly Colenso wanted to be known as the man who had discovered the moa. In 1841 he went down the east coast of North Islands, asking the Maoris if they could guide him to the whereabouts of the great bird. He did some digging and uncovered five moa thigh-bones, several smaller bones, and a bumper crop of Maori myths about the moa. When Colenso returned home in April of 1842, he shipped his finds to scientists in London, and wrote a blazing newspaper article denouncing everyone else who claimed to be the first to find the moa. He claimed that Joel Polack, the merchant who had published the earliest report on the big birds, was illiterate and could not have written anything. He swore that he knew nothing of Rule's bone or Owen's 1839 report on it. He insisted that he, and he alone, had been the first to find moa bones.

For many years the loud controversy between the pro-Colenso and anti-Colenso factions spread confusion over the discovery of the moa, but while the shouting continued Richard Owen quietly classified and reconstructed the moa bones. He gave the bird the scientific name of *Dinornis*, 'terrible bird', and declared that there had been at least five forms of moa. North Island had *Dinornis robustus*, the robust moa; *Dinornis elephantopus*, the elephant-footed moa; and *Dinornis crassus*, the fat moa. On South Island lived *Dinornis giganteus*, the giant moa; and *Dinornis gracilis*, the slender moa.

Many explorers joined the search for moa remains. The best finds were made by Walter Mantell, a government official whose father had been a famous palaeontologist and geologist. Between 1847 and 1850 Mantell collected a thousand separate bones on both islands, and fragments of eggshells that had been as much as ten inches long when they were whole. When this material reached London, Owen saw that there were six species of *Dinornis*, not five, and that there were fifteen or twenty other kinds of moa as well.

Zoologists today class the moa in five different genera, numbering more than twenty-four species all told. The smallest moa was about the size of a turkey, and the tallest was twice the size of a man. The bones were unusually thick and heavy; the elephant-footed moa, which was only five feet high, had such massive bones that it is hard to believe they belonged to a bird. Other moas were more slender, though none were exactly fragile-looking. In general appearance they were somewhat like ostriches, with long necks and small heads, rounded bodies, and huge powerful legs. The biggest moa of all, *Dinornis maximus*, was twelve feet tall – much bigger than any ostrich, and two feet taller even than the *Aepyornis* of

Madagascar. However, this was a relatively light-boned moa that probably weighed less than two-thirds as much as the stockier *Aepyornis*.

This array of monstrous birds, twenty or thirty types all told, had never existed in New Zealand all at one time. Some had been extinct for millions of years; others were quite recent. The oldest of the moa bones showed chemical changes that indicated an age of 15 to 35 million years. But most of the bones were not fossilized at all, and looked quite fresh. Which provoked some urgent questions. Was the moa totally extinct? If so, when and why had it died out? If not, where could living moas be found?

If anyone knew the answers to these questions, he was likely to be found among the Maoris. So the scientists turned to the natives of New Zealand for help.

The first explorer who had questioned a Maori about the wildlife of New Zealand was Captain Cook. In November 1769, he had spoken with a native chieftain, aided by an interpreter. He had learned of various unusual animals and recorded their description in his journal. The chief had not said a word about big birds. That was not a good sign to those who had turned to Cook's journal in hope of finding a clue to the existence of live moas.

In 1844, though, Governor FitzRoy of New Zealand questioned an old Maori named Haumatangi. He was about eighty-five, and claimed to remember the second visit of Captain Cook in 1773. Haumatangi said that the last moa in his part of New Zealand had been seen two hunts before Cook's arrival. Another elderly Maori, Kawana Papai, said he had personally taken part in moa hunts when he was a boy about 1790. He claimed that the birds were rounded up and killed with spears. It was a hazardous sport, because the moa defended itself with vigorous kicks; but it had to stand on one leg in order to kick with the other, and the Maori hunters brought it to the ground by aiming their blows against the leg it was standing on.

Several other Maoris came forward with stories of moa hunts on which they, their fathers, or their grandfathers had gone in the late eighteenth century. From this evidence it seemed that the last moa had been hunted to death about 1800. But how dependable were the memories of these old men? Perhaps they were simply inventing the stories for their own amusement and because it seemed to make the white men so happy to hear them.

Indeed, there was plenty of evidence of a negative kind. The Maori tales of the giant bird had too many mythological overtones, involving supernatural powers and mysterious traits. These fanciful legends aroused suspicion that the Maoris were embroidering on the discovery of the giant bones to make a good story better. It turned out that the word *moa* in the Maori language meant 'a stone' or 'a raised plot of land', and the big birds had actually been known as *tarepo*. It was developed that when a Maori declared, 'My grandfather said he hunted moas', he might really be saying 'My ancestor said he hunted moas', for the Maori words for 'grandfather' and 'ancestor' were the same. As for Colenso's name of moa, no one could be quite sure how it had become attached to the giant birds, but one story held that Colenso had asked the natives for 'more bones' and the Maoris, understanding this as 'moa bones', came to call the big birds by that name to please the Englishmen.

It was not at all certain, then, that the moas had survived until recent times, and most of the accounts by living Maoris of having seen moas were open to serious doubt. But it could not be doubted that man and moa had inhabited New Zealand at the same time. Charred moa bones were found in mounds near many native settlements. They were mainly the bones of the short, squat, heavy moa known as *Euryapteryx gravis*, which must have been prized for its meat. In 1859 miners discovered a Maori tomb which contained a skeleton in a sitting position; in the skeleton's hands, as though placed there for nourishment on the journey to the afterworld, was a whole *Dinornis* egg, ten inches long and seven inches wide. In later years, fossil hunters found moa bones that still contained muscles, ligaments, scraps of skin, and even some feathers. Obviously the moa had survived until recent times. But – how recent?

About 1870 an expedition led by Ferdinand von Hochstetter of Austria came to New Zealand to study the moa problem. Hochstetter talked to Maoris and to white settlers who claimed to have caught glimpses of fleeing moas in the jungles; he examined the testimony of the natives whose grandfathers had allegedly hunted the big birds; and he collected specimens. Hochstetter's verdict was that the Maoris had hunted the moa ever since the arrival of the Great Fleet about 1300. 'The natives ate the flesh and eggs,' he wrote, 'they adorned their hair with the feathers, crushed the skulls and tattooed themselves with the powder, made fish-hooks from the bones, and placed the giant eggs with the dead in their graves.' In fact, the moa had been the Maoris' chief source of food. 'But for these colossal birds,' he argued, 'it would be indeed utterly impossible to comprehend how 200,000 or 300,000 human beings could have lived in New Zealand, a country which even in its vegetable world offered nothing for subsistence, except fern-roots.'

He felt that the moas had been 'stupid, clumsy birds

. . . not swift runners like the ostrich, but sluggish diggers of the ground'. They had been easy to kill, and eventually the Maoris exterminated them all. That forced them to raise crops and livestock to survive, though Hochstetter also suggested that the end of the moas led the Maoris to turn towards cannibalism. He concluded that the age of moa remains 'can only be counted by hundreds, instead of thousands of years'.

As for the survival of the moa into modern times, Hochstetter doubted it. The big flightless birds that some people claimed to have seen, he said, were not moas, but

Kiwi

rather a large form of the wingless, hairy-looking little kiwi. He showed that the kiwi was really a tiny moa, structurally similar in everything but size. Hochstetter found fossil remains of a bird that could be considered either a very large kiwi or a very small moa. He felt that this medium-sized flightless bird might still be in existence, though the giant forms were gone.

Hochstetter's big kiwi has never been found alive, nor has anyone spotted a live moa. Most of his other ideas, though, have won general acceptance. It now seems clear that moas flourished in New Zealand for thousands of years, but were hunted to extermination by the Maoris between A.D. 1300 and A.D. 1800, with most of them probably gone by 1500 or so and only a few stragglers lingering after that time. When Captain Cook landed, the moas of North Island were extinct, which is why the Maoris he questioned there had never heard of the bird. Probably the South Island moas still provided feasts for the hunters for a time after Cook's visit. The big moas, being so conspicuous, must have been the first to go, but smaller forms such as *Euryapteryx* may well have endured into the nineteenth century.

Archaeologists conducting recent research in New Zealand have added some new twists to the moa problem. In 1939 excavations were begun in Pyramid Valley, a hundred miles inland from the north-east coast of South Island. Roger Duff and Robert Falla, two New Zealand scientists, found a sticky, muddy swamp there that had been a natural trap for moas. The heavy birds, venturing out on to the deceptive crust of the swamp, became mired in clay and could not get free. By 1949 Duff and Falla had uncovered the virtually complete skeletons of 140 moas, of four genera and six different species. Nearly a third were *Dinornis*, the tallest of the moas, and a dozen were *Euryapteryx*.

The archaeologists used a complex technique known as pollen dating to find out when these moas had perished. They discovered that the peat deposits underlying the swamp had been laid down about 1700 B.C. The moas themselves had tumbled into the swamp over a period of many centuries, beginning about A.D. 500. That was long

before any Maoris had arrived in New Zealand. But
some of the moas were preserved so well that the con-
tents of their stomachs lay with their skeletons. Seeds
and twigs that had been the last meal of a giant *Dinornis*
were subjected to the carbon-14 dating method, which
gave an age of about 670 years. That is, the biggest of the
moas had still been in existence in New Zealand about
the time the Maoris Great Fleet landed.

Duff also conducted excavations about a hundred
miles away, at Wairau, which showed the existence of a
pre-Maori people that hunted moas. At this ancient
camp, more than a thousand years old, moa bones were
found in profusion, along with moa eggs carefully per-
forated at one end as if they had been used as bottles.
Most of these moas were of the genus *Euryapteryx*, four
times as tall as a domestic chicken and packed solidly
with edible meat. No bones of *Dinornis*, the bird that has
sometimes been compared with the giraffe, were found in
this camp.

So the hunting of the moa began before the Maoris
came to New Zealand. The Maoris continued the slaughter. Probably the first to go was *Dinornis*, but even this
moa lasted until at least six hundred years ago. Carbon-
14 dating shows that some Maori objects made of the
skin and feathers of smaller moas were fashioned in the
eighteenth century.

Few people seriously expect to find the *Dinornis*
alive in New Zealand today, but the hope still burns that
one of the smaller moas may turn up. Sir George Grey,
who was Governor of New Zealand in the nineteenth
century reported in 1868 that he had met a party of
natives who gave him an account of the recent killing of
a small moa, 'describing with much spirit its capture out
of a drove of six or seven'. Sir George was a reliable in-

formant, but his native friends were not necessarily telling the truth. However, the place where the Maoris claimed they had hunted the moa later proved to shelter another New Zealand flightless bird that had likewise been believed extinct, the *takahe*. If that bird could reappear in one of the unexplored pockets of South Island, the argument goes, it is perfectly possible that a moa or two may be living there, too.

Maybe so. It would be delightful to read of the rediscovery of the moa, which no man has seen alive, so far as we can be sure, for more than two hundred years. Any moas that are found, though, will almost certainly be of the smaller types. The mighty *Dinornis*, like Madagascar's *Aepyornis*, is no more likely to be seen again than Sinbad's rukh, whose wings blotted out the sun and turned day into night.

8

The Giant Ground Sloth

One of the oddest of the world's living fossils is the tree sloth of South and Central America. These animals are about the size of large dogs, and spend virtually their entire lives hanging upside down from the limbs of trees. They have arms that are much longer than their legs and that are tipped with long, sharp, curving claws. A sloth digs into a branch and hangs on, eating, sleeping, and even nursing its babies while dangling upside down. Sloths have round heads, flat-featured faces, and dim little eyes. Their appearance is one of striking stupidity, and in this case appearance and substance are the same, for the tree sloth is a slow-moving, slow-witted animal with remarkably little intelligence. Sloths are so stupid that they hardly even seem to know when they have been seriously hurt. They show little sign of feeling pain, and can survive wounds that would kill many another animal.

A tree sloth gives the impression of being something ancient, a survivor from some remote era. That was Georges Cuvier's opinion, when sloth specimens were brought to that great French naturalist late in the eighteenth century. He called them 'relics of another order of things, the living remnants of an earlier state of nature ... creatures that by some miracle escaped the catastrophe which destroyed their contemporaries'. Cuvier's theory of catastrophes was rejected by science, but he was right about the ancestry of the tree sloth. These sluggish tropical animals are all that remain of what once was a large and widespread tribe.

The first fossil of an extinct sloth was found in 1789 on the banks of the River Lujan in Argentina. The Spanish viceroy at Buenos Aires had the bones dug out and shipped to Madrid, where a scholar named José Garriga set to work assembling and mounting them. Garriga spent six years preparing the specimen. News leaked out that the Spaniards had found some sort of gigantic monster, and, as the years passed without any report from Garriga, Cuvier, who had been nicknamed 'the pope of bones', felt that he had to know more about it. He persuaded a friend in Madrid to take an advance peep at Garriga's unfinished report. The friend not only got a copy of Garriga's paper, but even obtained a printer's proof of a picture of the skeleton. He smuggled these to Cuvier in Paris in 1795.

So it was Cuvier, somewhat unethically, who officially announced the giant ground sloth to science. He gave it the name of *Megatherium*, 'large mammal', and correctly identified it as a huge ground-dwelling relative of the tree sloth, as big as an elephant and far more massive. 'Its teeth,' wrote Cuvier, 'prove that it lived on vegetables, and its sturdy forefeet, armed with cutting claws, lead us to believe that it was principally their roots that it attacked. Its size and its foreclaws would have provided sufficient means of defence. It could not run fast, but it was not necessary for it to do so, as it had no need either to pursue or to flee.'

A year later, poor José Garriga at last felt ready to publish the report he had been so painstakingly pre-

Tree Sloth

paring for six years. Cuvier had stolen his thunder and even given his animal a scientific name, which should have been Garriga's privilege. But Garriga's paper gave a more complete description of the *Megatherium*. Since the idea of extinction was still quite new, and every unknown animal that came to light was a source of great wonder, the learned men of Europe buzzed over this monstrous beast that Cuvier said had lived before the deluge of Noah.

It was awesomely big. If it stood upright, it would have been fifteen feet high, but actually it walked in a slouching shuffle, leaning forward so that its head was usually about eight feet above the ground. It supported itself on its ponderous hind legs, balancing on an incredibly thick and heavy tail. The long forelimbs of the *Megatherium* were armed with ferocious claws like a row of sickles. Looking a little like a colossal hairy bear, the giant ground sloth shambled along from tree to tree, using its paws to claw down the tender top branches, and munching on leaves and twigs. When it had browsed on all the foliage within easy reach, it might lean its weight against a taller tree and uproot it for its next meal. At least, it was strong enough to do that, though if it were as sluggish as its present-day cousins, it probably did not make the effort.

The excitement caused by the discovery of the first giant ground sloth set in motion a wave of new digging. Thomas Jefferson, exploring a cave in Virginia, found the fossil remains of a different, though equally gigantic, ground sloth. Soon half a dozen types were known. One was *Mylodon robustus*, which was about eleven feet long and differed from the *Megatherium* mainly in having arms and legs of the same length; the *Megatherium*'s legs were much shorter than its arms. Then came *Mylodon gracilis*, which means 'the dainty *Mylodon*', but *gracilis* was 'dainty' only by comparison with *robustus*. This delicate, slender *Mylodon* was a nine-footer that weighed many tons. Other ground sloths included *Glossotherium*, *Megalonyx*, *Grypotherium*, *Lestodon*, and *Hapalops* – a grotesque menagerie of clumsy colossi, some no bigger than bears, others heavier than rhinoceroses or elephants. They all were vegetarians, all were heavy-boned and huge, and all lived in warm climates, from the southern part of North America down through Central and South America.

The giant ground sloths had one other thing in common. They were all extinct.

King Charles IV of Spain was so impressed by the *Megatherium* at Madrid that he ordered his officials in the New World to send him a ground sloth at once, dead or alive. The monarch's request had to go unfulfilled. No doubt the colonial administrators in South America looked far and wide for a live *Megatherium*, but none were available.

By the middle of the nineteenth century, the old ideas about the age of the world had generally been rejected, and a clear picture of evolution and extinction had emerged. It was realized that the giant ground sloths belonged to a group of large mammals that had inhabited both the Americas millions of years ago. The ground sloths and such other creatures as the glyptodont, a giant armadillo, and the toxodon, a rhinoceros-like animal, had originated in South America at a time when that continent was cut off by water from North America. There were no beasts of prey in South America then, so huge, sluggish plant-eating animals could flourish there in peace. When the Americas finally became joined by the land bridge of Central America, the big beasts of South America came north, but also the tigers, dogs, bears, and other predatory animals of the north went south. Many of the South American animals, unable to compete in the new environment, died out.

The giant sloth and the giant armadillo seem to have survived, though, for quite a while – the sloth because it was so big, the armadillo because its round shell made it virtually an armoured tank. When men first entered the Americas, these big animals still were found in the warmer regions.

That man, *Megatherium*, and glyptodont existed at

the same time was repeatedly proved in the nineteenth century. Indian drawings of the giant sloths and armadillos were discovered, as well as ancient camp-sites at which the blackened bones of *Mylodon* testified to lavish feasts. In 1881 a South American investigator came upon a burial deposit in which a human skeleton lay curled up under the domelike shell of a giant armadillo. An Argentine palaeontologist, Florentino Ameghino, found a prize exhibit soon after: a *Megatherium* that had obviously been trapped by men and roasted for dinner in the pit where it had been caught.

No one could doubt that prehistoric man had hunted and eaten the giant ground sloth and the giant armadillo, five or ten thousand years ago. But when had the last hunt taken place? A thousand years ago? A hundred? Or was the giant ground sloth still alive somewhere in South America?

Florentino Ameghino appointed himself a one-man committee to prove that the ground sloth was not yet extinct. He was a reputable scientist, the leading palaeontologist of South America. But, like many scholars who begin with a preconceived idea and set out to find evidence to prove it, rather than beginning with the evidence and drawing conclusions from what they see, Ameghino was soon hip-deep in controversy and his reputation was tarnished by some of his claims.

Until 1898 his research on the giant ground sloth had taken the form of discovering its fossil remains, often charred or bearing other signs of association with man. In that year, though, he was given a specimen that set him on a new path.

A retired German sea captain named Eberhard had bought a ranch in southern Patagonia. Hanging over some bushes at this ranch was the hide of a large animal.

Captain Eberhard's visitors studied the hide with interest, because it was rough and bumpy, and seemed to be studded with bean-sized 'bones'. The hide was so tough that cutting it was difficult, but someone sliced off a small piece and sent it to Ameghino at the Buenos Aires Museum.

Ameghino recognized it at once as ground-sloth hide. Several types of ground sloth, including the *Mylodon* but not the *Megatherium*, had had skins containing these little bony lumps. Ameghino, in the course of his excavations of fossil sloths, had seen such hides many times. But those hides showed signs of great age. This bumpy fragment looked like part of the hide of an animal that had been killed and skinned a few years ago.

A short time before, Ameghino's friend, Ramón Lista, a former Argentine Secretary of State, had claimed to have seen a hairy animal of an unfamiliar type while hunting in southern Patagonia. It had had a thick tail on which it balanced, strong hind legs, and forearms tipped with powerful claws. Lista had fired a few shots at the beast, hitting it several times, but it had escaped as though the bullets had scarcely injured it. It was his opinion that he had seen a small ground sloth whose thick, bony hide had repelled his bullets. No one else shared this belief; even Ameghino believed that Lista had been 'the victim of an illusion'.

But now Ameghino was in possession of a strip of what he was sure was the hide of a recently killed ground sloth. If one ground sloth still existed in Patagonia, there might be two. Abruptly he changed his mind about the animal Lista had seen. It must have been a modern *Mylodon*, Ameghino announced at a large press conference. He went so far as to give it a scientific name, *Neomylodon listai*, 'Lista's new *Mylodon*'. Since Lista had recently been killed by Indians while on another exploring trip, he was unable to appreciate the honour.

The bit of hide was sufficient proof to Ameghino that ground sloths still existed in Patagonia. He repeated the idea in a long series of scientific papers, and turned his energies to uncovering further data. What he wanted, of course, was a live *Mylodon* or *Megatherium* that he could show a sceptical world. But finding one was not so easy.

Mylodon

While Ameghino was trying to resurrect the ground sloth, other scientists were checking up on Captain Eberhard's strange hide.

A Swedish archaeologist, Otto Nordenskjöld, had visited Eberhard in 1896 and received a small piece of the hide as a souvenir. Eberhard told Nordenskjöld that he and some friends had found the skin in 1859 in a large cave near the Patagonian coast. It had been five feet long and about half as wide, and had carefully been rolled up inside out and buried in the floor of the cave. A human skeleton lay nearby in a little niche.

Nordenskjöld carried out a partial excavation of the

cave where the hide had been found, and came upon the horny sheath of a *Mylodon's* huge claw. He took this and his piece of hide to Sweden, where they were studied by Einar Lönnberg, an expert on ground sloths. In 1899 Lönnberg published his report. He agreed with Ameghino that the bony hide and the claw had come from a ground sloth of the *Mylodon* group. But he saw no reason to believe that the animal still existed. 'It is absolutely impossible to think that this animal, if it was still among living beings, could have eluded the sharp eyes of the native Indians,' Lönnberg concluded. They would surely have been familiar with its tracks and would have noticed the places where it had broken off branches in its feeding. What Lönnberg did not know – and what excited Ameghino tremendously – was the fact that the Patagonian Indians *did* have legends of just such an animal.

Ameghino had carried out an extensive investigation into these Indian legends. He had heard from the Indians of a big four-legged beast called the *iemisch*, or 'water-tiger', which spent most of its time hiding in lakes, coming forth to seize, drown, and eat horses. The natives described the iemisch as having 'a short head, big canine teeth, and no external ears'. Its tail was long and flat, its hair was short and coarse, and its feet were armed with formidable claws. It was supposedly about the size of a puma.

The iemisch was said to be a flesh-eater; and Ameghino surely knew that all the sloths had been peaceful vegetarians. Perhaps the real iemisch was a jaguar, an animal that eats meat and swims well; or perhaps it was the giant river otter of South America, another aquatic carnivore. Its habits certainly did not fit those of any likely sloth. But someone had given Ameghino a translation of the word *iemisch*: 'the one with little stones on it'. He immediately conjured up the image of *Neomylodon listai*'s bumpy hide. That was good enough for Ameghino, who willingly closed his eyes to the rest of the legend and forced himself to swallow the fantastic notion of a carnivorous sloth.

Ameghino now began questioning the Indians about the iemisch. They told him endless stories about this mythical beast. Some of them even claimed to have killed iemisches recently. Meanwhile Captain Eberhard's cave was getting a careful going-over by a number of scientists. A Swedish party arrived in 1898 under Erland Nordenskjöld, Otto's cousin, and excavated more hide and some bones. Erland Nordenskjöld, after close study, declared that the animal of the cave had been a known extinct form, *Glossotherium darwini*, and so there had been no need for Ameghino to invent the name *Neomylodon listai*. Ameghino, who loved to coin scientific names, shot back that his animal was different, but he was starting to let his theories get in the way of his observations.

In the spring of 1899 an Argentine expedition led by the geologist Rudolf Hauthal went thoroughly over the cave and found an inner chamber surrounded by a crude wall of rough boulders. In this chamber were the signs of a prehistoric kitchen: charred pieces of bone, mussel shells, and the like. Underneath it was a mass of dung belonging to some plant-eating animal. Nearby was a heap of dry hay. Mixed in with the hay and dung were the broken bones of the *Glossotherium* or *Neomylodon*. Another rolled-up hide was found in the rear.

The bones, the dung, and the hay indicated clearly that at some time in the past this cave had served both as a pen and as a slaughter-house for giant ground sloths.

The animals had been kept alive and provided with fodder until they were due for eating. Then they had been killed – the skulls had been broken with large stones – and cooked right in the cave. Dr Hauthal concluded that 'the men who lived there ages ago were accustomed to stable their domestic animals in this part of the cavern, reserving the rest for their own dwelling place'. Other scholars agreed. A study of the dung showed that the sloths had eaten the hay, which had been cut and stacked by human beings. Perhaps it was going a little too far to call this a 'stable' and to term the sloths 'domestic animals'. More likely, they had been driven into the cave and held prisoner there, and not raised in captivity. After all, if sloths had really been domestic animals for the Indians, they would not have become extinct. No animal is less likely to become extinct than one that is bred in captivity by man.

However, the evidence of the cave proved once again that man and giant ground sloth had been contemporaries. That had been known for some time. But the legend of the iemisch entered to confuse matters here.

Among the sloth bones in the cave, there had also been found a leg bone of a jaguar-like animal. Santiago Roth, Hauthal's colleague on the expedition, instantly suggested that this was a bone of the carnivorous iemisch. Ameghino came right back with an attack on this idea. The iemisch, he still insisted, was a ground sloth related to *Mylodon*, and no jaguar at all. In an article published in 1900 Ameghino described his *Neomylodon*, or iemisch, as an animal 'as big as a large ox with shorter legs ... it is about a third smaller than *Mylodon robustus*. Its body is covered with long, thick, coarse hair ... The very thick skin bears little bones identical to those in the fossil genus *Mylodon* ... The head is longer than the *My-*

lodon's, ending in a pointed snout, and the external ears are only rudimentary ... The feet are flat; the toes are joined by a swimming membrane, and also armed with large sickle-like claws as in *Glossotherium, Catonyx,* and *Mylodon*.'

Ameghino, who should have known better, was now presenting a very unattractive spectacle: that of the scientist who turns facts upside down to fit a theory. He began with a bony piece of hide, an Indian legend, and a conviction that giant ground sloths still existed. In order to cling to that conviction and make the iemisch legend hang together with the fossil evidence, he found himself forced to turn the clumsy, land-dwelling, leaf-eating ground sloth into a swift swimmer that hunted and devoured horses.

Early in the twentieth century several other scientists devoted some time to tracking down the origin of the iemisch story. They showed that the iemisch probably was mythical, combining the fierceness of the jaguar with the swimming abilities of the river otter. Except for the claws it was said to have, it bore no resemblance whatever to anything that could have been considered a ground sloth. That disposed of one of Ameghino's pet ideas. The iemisch was not a *Neomylodon*. But even so, did the *Neomylodon* exist, or was it extinct?

Ameghino dug into the accounts of earlier naturalists. An eighteenth-century book by Father Pedro Lozano, a Portuguese priest, mentioned a Patagonian animal called the *su*, or *succarath*. It was described as a large, savage beast that had the habit of carrying its young on its back. The natives supposedly hunted it for its hide, which was used for cloaks. Since existing sloths carry their young on their backs, Ameghino decided that the su must be a sloth, too – perhaps his *Neomylodon*.

He went back further, to a work by the sixteenth-century Swiss naturalist, Conrad Gesner. His great book, the *Historia Animalium* (1551–58), was a summary of all zoological knowledge of that day. Gesner mentioned the su also, and said it was found at the southern end of South America – that is, Patagonia. The Patagonians made cloaks from its hide, said Gesner. 'It is very dreadful, obnoxious, as may be seen,' he wrote. 'When hunted by the hunters, it takes its young upon its back, covers them with its long tail, and thus flees. It is caught in pits and killed with arrows.'

From Gesner, Ameghino went to Gesner's original source, the *Description of America* of André Thévet. Thévet's book, published in 1558, was one of the first to deal with the natural history of the New World, and Gesner had drawn liberally on it. According to Thévet, the su 'lives for most of the time on the banks of rivers . . . The savages use a trick to catch this beast: making a deep pit near the place where it is in the habit of making its abode, and covering it with green leaves, so that when running, without suspecting the ambush, the poor beast falls in this pit with its young. When it seems that it is caught, it maims and kills its young (as if maddened): and gives such terrible cries that it makes the savages very fearful and timid. Yet in the end they kill it with arrows and then they flay it.'

Just what the su really was, no one is quite sure. Ameghino, of course, maintained that it was *Neomylodon*. Perhaps so, although a cloak made from the hide of that animal would have weighed fifty pounds or so. Possibly it was used for armour, though. There is no reason to disagree with Ameghino's conclusion that the su was a small ground sloth that was still hunted in Patagonia as late as the sixteenth century. Since we have ample proof that man did hunt ground sloths there for thousands of years, we cannot deny that a few sloths may have lived on into recent times.

But that does not mean that there are any giant ground sloths today.

Ameghino's vigorous propaganda campaign aroused widespread public interest in this animal at the beginning of this century. Undeniably it was exciting to think that a huge, shaggy creature of remote antiquity might still roam the unexplored wildernesses of distant Patagonia. It was still easy to believe that dinosaurs and other long-extinct animals might be found in Africa or South America; and if dinosaurs, then why not a *Mylodon* or two?

A London newspaper organized an expedition to Patagonia before the First World War. Its leader, Hesketh H. Pritchard, seems to have been a hotheaded, short-tempered man. Soon after the expedition reached South America, Pritchard announced loudly that he had been hoaxed and that the *iemisch* was a myth. Everything concerned with the ground sloth, Pritchard said, was dishonest. Without even bothering to enter Patagonia, he turned back denouncing the whole enterprise.

Two later expeditions showed greater patience, but even so they found no *Mylodons*. There were some promising rumours – one explorer saw 'two bears walking upright with faces like men', another came upon mounds of giant sloths' dung that seemed to be fresh – but none of these stories led to a discovery. A scientific report written in 1949 summed up the situation by declaring that there were many 'more or less trustworthy reports about the existence of a large animal in certain lakes in the mountains to the west', but that no evidence more tangible than that had been gathered.

Carbon-14 dating indicates that man hunted ground sloths in Patagonia about ten thousand years ago. Other information leads us to suspect that man was still hunting ground sloths in Patagonia as recently as four hundred years ago. More than that we cannot say. Probably the ground sloths were already well on the way to extinction when man first reached the Americas. They were slow, dim animals of an earlier era, moving along the downward curve of their race. Very likely their birth rate was low and only their great bulk, protecting them from attackers, kept them from extinction. When human hunters launched a campaign against them, their numbers dwindled until they reached the zero point.

The South American jungles have yielded many strange creatures thought to be extinct. Perhaps a live *Mylodon* or *Megatherium* will come shambling out of the woods some day. Florentino Ameghino to the contrary, though, it seems unlikely that any of these hairy giants still survive.

9

The Passenger Pigeon
and the Heath Hen

When European explorers reached eastern North America in the sixteenth century, they were astonished by the flocks of birds they saw in the virgin forests. Coming from a continent that had already cut down most of its forest land, they found it incredible that so many millions upon millions of birds could be seen.

One American bird in particular taxed their powers of belief. It was a large, handsome pigeon, sometimes eighteen inches long from beak to tail, that nested in the northern forests in summer and flew south in cold weather. The male pigeons were unusually beautiful, with rich, glossy-blue plumage on their wings and backs, and breasts of a wine-red chestnut hue, fading to white underneath the tail. Iridescent spots of bronze and green gave a brilliant sheen to their necks, and their eyes, a bright, fiery orange, were strangely vivid. The females were less colourful, as is true with many birds; they were light brown above, grey below, and lacking in the males' shining highlights of bronze.

It was not the beauty but the abundance of these birds that startled the explorers. At nesting time the pigeons gathered in enormous flocks, settling in breeding colonies that could stretch over forest areas three miles wide and thirty miles long. Their nests were densely packed, often a hundred to a tree, so that the boughs groaned under the weight and frequently broke off, falling to the ground with a crash. Some of these miles-long nesting areas contained 30 to 50 million birds. Their voices were loud and raucous; anyone who came within a few miles of a nesting area might think that he was hearing the croaking of a giant army of bullfrogs. In the forests, pigeon droppings covered the ground to a depth of several inches, killing every plant, and the trees were stripped of their leaves. When the flock moved on, it left a scene of awesome devastation behind.

Seeing millions of these birds camped in a forest must have been disturbing and a little frightening, for the noise was so great, the odour so fierce, the general appearance of the scene so weird and strange. But what must have been truly awesome was the sight of these vast flocks taking to the air on their annual migrations. Their beating wings eclipsed the sun, and created a sound like the roaring of a waterfall or the rumbling of distant thunder.

The French explorer Samuel de Champlain wrote in 1605 of 'an infinite number of pigeons' he had seen along the coast of Maine. Another Frenchman, Josselyn, wrote in 1672, 'I have seen a flight of pigeons that to my thinking had neither beginning nor ending, length nor breadth, and so thick I could not see the sun.' Naturalists came to study these phenomenal aggregations of birds. Because the pigeons were birds of passage, or migratory birds, they became known as *passenger pigeons*.

Mark Catesby, who wrote *The Natural History of Carolina, Florida, and the Bahama Islands* in 1731, declared: 'Of these pigeons there come in Winter to *Virginia* and *Carolina* from the North, incredible Numbers; insomuch that in some places where they roost (which they do on one another's Backs) they often break down the limbs of Oaks with their weight, and leave their Dung some Inches thick under the Trees they roost on. Where they light, they so effectually clear the Woods of Acorns ... that the Hogs that come after them ... fare very poorly. In *Virginia* I have seen them fly in such continued trains three days successively, that there was not the least Interval in losing sight of them, but that some where or other in the Air they were to be seen continuing their flight South ...'

A Scottish ornithologist who went to the United States early in the nineteenth century, Alexander Wilson, visited a nesting site of passenger pigeons in Kentucky that covered some 120 square miles. He studied the ruin caused by the birds – the broken boughs strewn about as though after a hurricane, the mounds of dung, the trees 'killed as completely as if girdled with an axe'. It took years, Wilson said, for a forest to return to its green state after passenger pigeons had nested there.

'Almost every tree was furnished with nests,' he wrote, 'wherever the branches could accommodate them ... As soon as the young were fully grown, and before they left the nests, numerous parties of the inhabitants, from all parts of the adjacent country, came with wagons, axes, beds, cooking utensils, many of them accompanied by the greater part of their families, and encamped for several days by this immense nursery. Several of them informed me, that the noise in the woods was so great as to terrify their horses, and that it was difficult for one person to hear another speak without bawling in his ear. The ground was strewed with broken limbs of trees, eggs, and young squab Pigeons, which had been precipitated from above, and on which herds of hogs were fattening. Hawks, Buzzards, and Eagles were sailing about in great

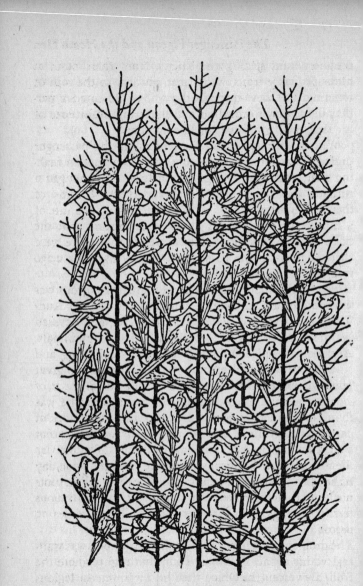

Passenger Pigeons

numbers, and seizing the squabs from their nests at pleasure; while from twenty feet upwards to the tops of the trees the view through the woods presented a perpetual tumult of crowding and fluttering multitudes of pigeons, their wings roaring like thunder.'

Wilson later watched a flock of migrating passenger pigeons in action. When he first heard the 'sudden rushing roar, succeeded by instant darkness', he thought a tornado was beginning. Wilson observed a column of flying pigeons more than a mile wide moving at a rate of a mile a minute for four hours, which meant that the flock was 240 miles long. He calculated that there were three pigeons to the cubic yard in the flight, or 2,230 million in the entire flock.

The most famous description of passenger pigeons was written by the French-born naturalist John James Audubon, who settled in Pennsylvania in 1803 and devoted his life to the study of American birds and mammals. Audubon travelled through the country collecting and studying wildlife and making the sketches for two great books of plates, *Birds of America* and *Quadrupeds of North America*. In the autumn of 1813, when he was living in Henderson, Kentucky, Audubon saw a flock of passenger pigeons flying south-west in numbers that were amazing even for passenger pigeons. 'The air was literally filled with Pigeons,' he wrote, 'and the noon-day light was obscured as by an eclipse. The dung fell in spots not unlike melting flakes of snow; and the continuous buzz of wings had a tendency to lull my senses to repose.'

Riding on some fifty miles farther, Audubon was waiting for his dinner at Young's Inn that night, where the Salt River meets the Ohio, when he saw 'immense legions still going by. Their front reached far beyond the Ohio on the west, and the beechwood forests directly east of me. Not a single bird alighted, for not a nut or acorn was that year to be seen in the neighbourhood ... I cannot describe to you the extreme beauty of their aerial evolutions when a Hawk chanced to press upon the rear of a flock. At once, like a torrent, and with a noise like thunder, they rushed in a compact mass, pressing upon each other towards the centre. In these almost solid masses they darted forward in undulating and angular lines, descended to the earth and swept close over it with inconceivable velocity. Then they mounted perpendicularly so as to resemble a vast column, and, when high, they were seen wheeling and twisting within their continued lines, which resembled the coils of a gigantic serpent.'

Audubon was struck by the 'rapidity and elegance of the motions'. He wrote: 'As soon as the Pigeons discover a sufficiency of food to entice them to alight, they fly around in circles, reviewing the countryside below. During these evolutions the dense mass which they form presents a beautiful spectacle, as it changes its direction, turning from a glistening sheet of azure, as the backs of the birds come simultaneously into view, to a suddenly presented, rich deep purple. After that they pass lower, over the woods, and for a moment are lost among the foliage. Again they emerge and glide aloft. They may now alight, but the next moment take to wing as if suddenly alarmed, the flapping of their wings producing a noise like the roar of distant thunder, as they sweep through the forests to see if danger is near. However, hunger soon brings them to the ground.'

Like all other observers, Audubon was awed by the destruction a flock of 50 million passenger pigeons would work as it passed its six-week nesting period in a forest. He wrote of fallen branches and stripped trees and woods smothered in dung. But a different kind of destruction was also to be seen: the mass slaughter of the pigeons.

Their meat was highly edible, and whenever the flocks passed overhead on their yearly migrations the hunters came forth. Audubon tells how on one flight in 1813 the pigeons flew over Kentucky for three days in succession: 'The people were all in arms, and the banks of the Ohio were crowded with men and boys incessantly shooting at the pilgrims, which flew lower as they passed the river. Multitudes were thus destroyed. For a week or more, the population fed on no other flesh than that of Pigeons, and talked of nothing but Pigeons.'

Aiming a shotgun towards the heavens and bringing down a batch of birds with every blast was easy enough, but it was easier still to kill the pigeons in their dense forest gatherings. The nesting time of the passenger pigeons was feasting time for the people of the eastern United States. Audubon wrote:

'A great gathering of persons with horses and wagons, guns and ammunition had pitched camp on the edge of the forest. Two farmers from the vicinity of Russellville, more than a hundred miles distant, had driven more than three hundred hogs to be fattened on the Pigeons they hoped to slaughter. Here and there, people were busy plucking and salting birds already killed, and they sat amid large piles of them ... I noticed that many trees two feet in diameter were broken off at no great distance from the ground; and the branches of many of the largest and tallest had given way. It was as if the forest had been swept by a tornado, proving to me that the number of birds must be immense beyond conception.

'As the time of the arrival of the Passenger Pigeons approached, their foes anxiously prepared to receive them. Some persons were ready with iron pots containing sulphur, others with torches of pine knots; many had poles, and the rest, guns. The sun went down, yet not a Pigeon had arrived. However, everything was ready, and all eyes were fixed on the clear sky which could be glimpsed amid the tall tree-tops.

'Suddenly a general cry burst forth, "Here they come!" The noise they made, even though still distant, reminded me of a hard gale at sea, passing through the rigging of a close-reefed vessel. As the birds arrived and passed over me, I felt a current of air that surprised me. Thousands of the Pigeons were soon knocked down by the pole-men, while more continued to pour in. The fires were lighted, then a magnificent, wonderful, and almost terrifying sight presented itself. The Pigeons, arriving by the thousands, alighted everywhere, one above another, until solid masses were formed on the branches all around. Here and there the perches gave way with a crash under the weight, and fell to the ground, destroying hundreds of birds beneath, and forcing down the dense groups of them with which every stick was loaded. The scene was one of uproar and confusion. I found it quite useless to speak, or even to shout, to those persons nearest me. Even the gun reports were seldom heard, and I was made aware of the firing only by seeing the shooters reloading.

'No one dared venture nearer the devastation. Meanwhile, the hogs had been penned up. The picking up of the dead and wounded birds was put off till morning. The Pigeons were constantly coming, and it was past midnight before I noticed any decrease in the number of those arriving. The uproar continued the whole night. I was anxious to know how far away the sound could be heard, so I sent off a man used to roaming the forest, who returned in two hours with the information that he had heard it distinctly three miles from the roosting place.

'Towards the approach of day, the noise somewhat subsided. Long before I could distinguish them plainly, the Pigeons began to move off in a direction quite different from the one in which they flew when they arrived the evening before. By sunrise all that were able to fly had disappeared. The howling of the wolves now reached our ears, and the foxes, lynxes, cougars, bears, raccoons, opossums and polecats were sneaking off. Eagles and Hawks, accompanied by a crowd of Vultures, took their place and enjoyed their share of the spoils.

'Then the authors of all this devastation began to move among the dead, the dying, and the mangled, picking up the Pigeons and piling them in heaps. When each man had as many as he could possibly dispose of, the hogs were let loose to feed on the remainder.'

Such indiscriminate killing, someone surely must have realized, would end with the extinction of the birds. But that seemed impossible; there were so many. Even Audubon, after viewing the holocaust of death, wrote: 'Persons unacquainted with these birds might naturally conclude that such dreadful havoc would soon put an end to the species. But I have satisfied myself, by long observation, that nothing but the gradual diminution of our forests can accomplish their decrease.'

The passenger pigeon, though, was not immune to extinction. Severe overhunting had already reduced their numbers in certain localities. As early as 1672, a New England settler noted that 'of late they [the pigeons] are much diminished, the English taking them with nets'. The Indians, who used the fat of the passenger pigeon as butter, valued the birds highly and were careful not to kill adult birds while they were raising their young, since that would leave the fledglings to starve, a costly waste.

But the white men were not so cautious. The pigeons seemed without limit, so it was foolish to take conservation measures. Mark Catesby wrote in 1731 how even 'the People of *New York* and *Philadelphia* shoot many of them as they fly by, from their Balconies and Tops of Houses; and in *New-England* there are such Numbers, that with long Poles they knock them down from their Roosts in the Night in great numbers'.

Neither in forest nor in city was the passenger pigeon safe from hunters. The sparse tribes of Indians could not make serious inroads into the population of birds, nor could the early white settlers kill enough birds to hurt the species. But in the nineteenth century, when the United States began to grow, the passenger pigeon showed the effects of the slaughter. In 1800 the population of the United States was 5,297,000, and the passenger pigeons numbered in thousands of millions. By 1900 there were 76,094,000 Americans, and virtually no passenger pigeons at all. Within that century, a species that represented twenty-five to forty per cent of the entire bird population of the United States was destroyed.

Audubon, in 1805, saw thousands of dead passenger pigeons being unloaded on the Hudson River docks of New York City, where they were sold for a cent apiece. But a few years later the birds were a fashionable delicacy in great demand, and the price rose to one dollar a dozen. That made it profitable to hunt them, and the huge massacres commenced. Professional pigeon hunters followed the birds from one breeding ground to the next, shooting, clubbing, and netting. One man Audubon saw in action claimed to kill more than 10,000 pigeons a day, sometimes netting several hundred in a single cast of his net. A common practice was to cut down the trees in which the birds nested, to get at the tender young squabs. Tons of passenger pigeons streamed to market; the craving for them seemed to be as bottomless as the supply.

Not only was the passenger pigeon desired for the table, but it also figured in what was known as sport. Thousands of live pigeons were trapped and kept in boxes for pigeon hunts. Then they were released, as living targets for the rifles of fashionable stockbrokers, lawyers, doctors, and their wives. These pigeon shoots were elaborate social events of the time.

Despite the killing, the passenger pigeon did not show any great reduction in numbers during the early nineteenth century. When a Bill to protect the birds was proposed in Ohio in 1857, a committee of the state legislature reported, 'The passenger pigeon needs no protection. Wonderfully prolific – no ordinary destruction can lessen them.'

That was true. What happened to the passenger pigeon was extraordinary destruction.

The country was growing. Population doubled between 1800 and 1820, and doubled again by 1845, reaching 20 million. By 1860 there were 30 million Americans, 40 million by 1870. Cities were reaching out in all directions. Railway lines crisscrossed the continent. The forests were coming down.

The last factor was important in the decline of the passenger pigeon. As whole forests vanished, the breeding cycle of the birds was disrupted. They had to find new routes for their migrations. The acorns, nuts, and wild fruits on which they fed were harder to obtain. The passenger pigeons were extremely rigid in their habits, moving in fixed patterns, and they could not easily adapt to these changes. They became confused and troubled by the alterations in their accustomed way of life; and when animals are confused and troubled, it tends to have a negative effect on their fertility.

The fertility of the passenger pigeon had never been very great, anyway. That seems like a paradoxical statement, considering the vast numbers of the birds. But each pair of birds produced only one egg at a time – always a risky proposition for a species. Some animals are numerous because they have many offspring; the secret of the passenger pigeon's profusion was simply an absence of natural enemies. The birds had a continent to themselves, with an ideal supply of food and nothing to worry about except an occasional hawk or eagle. Once man began knocking passenger pigeons out of the sky by the millions, though, the scales began to tip towards extinction. The remaining pigeons, with their one fledgling a year, could not replace the losses.

It took several centuries of really dedicated destruction before the effects became visible. If a population of birds is reduced from 10 billion to 2 billion, it has suffered an 80-per-cent loss; but 2 billion birds are still a lot of birds. Between 1866 and 1876, 10 million pigeons a year were shipped to the eastern cities for food, and probably as many more were wounded and left to die in the woods, or starved to death when their parents were slain. Yet millions of the pigeons remained.

As the individual flocks were wiped out, the states belatedly got around to passing protective laws. New York State prohibited the hunting of passenger pigeons in 1867, Massachusetts in 1870, Pennsylvania in 1878. By then, though, the birds were rarely seen in those eastern states. Only in the Midwest did they still gather in any quantities.

The last of the great pigeon hunts took place near Petoskey, Michigan, in 1878. A mighty flock nested there in a forest range 28 miles long. The main body of birds – nearly a thousand million of them – occupied a compact mass a mile wide and 5 miles in length. The hunters moved in and killed 300 tons of birds in a month. Five freight-car loads of pigeons were shipped out every day for thirty days.

Smaller nesting grounds still could be found, and wherever the birds collected in numbers, they were hunted. About a million pigeons were discovered nesting in Michigan in 1881; during the hunt, fire broke out in the dry birch woods, and many of the birds perished in the flames. A later nesting in 1881, one in Pennsylvania in 1886, and one in Canada in 1887 also drew the hunters. But the passenger pigeon was becoming a scarce bird. The extent of the hunts, the felling of the forests, and the disruption of breeding habits had combined to thin the incredible swarms to a few scattered flocks.

After 1893, when the last commercial hunt took place, it no longer paid to kill the pigeons. So few of them were left that it was unprofitable to organize a hunting party. It might seem that once the hunting ended, the passenger pigeon would have been able to replenish its numbers, but that did not happen. The decline was irreversible. Evidently it was a bird that could thrive only in flocks of many millions; a few thousand isolated passenger pigeons, deprived of the raucous companionship of their comrades, were bewildered and lost. The survivors laid fewer eggs. Local hunters, potting a few birds every now and then, reduced their numbers still further. The harsh winters of the Canadian woods, where the pigeons had taken refuge after the destruction of the forests of the United States, brought more fatalities. As a species, the passenger pigeon had been brought to the point of no return.

Chief Pokagon of the Potawatomi Indians of Michigan found the last breeding colony in 1896 at the headwaters of the Au Sable River, in the north-central part of the Michigan peninsula. It numbered a few dozen pairs of birds. Pokagon, who had seen not only animals but his own race hunted by the white-skinned invaders of the continent, felt a special kinship for these last wild passenger pigeons, for he himself was the last chief of his tribe.

The birds that still survived were broken up into small bands that scattered widely over the continent. Never again were they seen to come together in breeding colonies. A few pigeons were seen in Illinois, Nebraska, and Wisconsin in the 1890s. They were found by hunters who shot them. Some 140 birds were seen – and killed – in Arkansas in 1902. A passenger pigeon was observed in Bar Harbour, Maine, in 1904. It was shot. A passenger pigeon was shot on the Black River of Arkansas in 1906. On 23 September 1907 a passenger pigeon was seen at St Vincent, Quebec. It, too, was brought down, of course. The man who shot it had a special distinction: no one else would ever be able to slay a wild passenger pigeon, for there were none left.

The species was not quite extinct, however. Very late in the day, a few passenger pigeons had been captured for zoos. Even after the Petoskey massacre of 1878, few people had been able to believe that this bird was actually headed towards extinction. There had always been so many of them that a total disappearance was as unthinkable as a total disappearance of ants or bees. Though the passenger pigeons had gone from many regions, it was easy to assume that they had simply moved somewhere else. By the time the truth was known, it was too late to save the passenger pigeon as the American bison had been saved.

Only a few pairs of the birds were kept in captivity. They bred slowly, and some did not breed at all. The older birds died faster than the young ones were born. Eventually just one passenger pigeon remained. Her name was Martha, and she lived in the Cincinnati Zoological Gardens: a slender grey and brown pigeon, who had been born in the zoo in 1885. Her cage was a place of special pilgrimage to many Americans, who came to stare in sorrow and curiosity at this last of all the passenger pigeons.

Rarely has the extinction of a species been so precisely recorded. Martha died on 1 September 1914 at 1 p.m., at the age of twenty-nine. Her body, packed in ice, was shipped to the United States National Museum in Washington to be dissected and mounted for display. Exactly 101 years earlier, John James Audubon had stood in an autumn-tinged Kentucky forest to stare in amazement at a flock of pigeons so numerous that 'the noon-day light was obscured as by an eclipse'.

The passenger pigeon was the most spectacular casualty of the unrestrained hunting in nineteenth-century America, because it outnumbered any other species of bird in the world, and yet was utterly eliminated within two or three generations. If it is hard to imagine the enormous size of the passenger pigeon flocks in Audubon's day, it is even harder to comprehend so rapid an extinction.

There were many other victims, though, during the same period. It was as if millions of men and boys had been turned loose in the American forests with the single aim of shooting at anything that flew, ran, crawled, or hopped. If it was edible or had valuable fur or decorative feathers, fine. If it had no particular commercial value, it was shot anyway, just for target practice.

Among the casualties was the heath hen, the eastern form of the prairie chicken. These birds are grouped with such game fowls as the grouse, and once were widespread in much of North America. The prairie chicken, which is not extinct, inhabits the plains west of the Mississippi from Texas to Canada. It has a tuft of ten or more round-tipped feathers at its neck, is brown with buff stripes, and lives in the open country, feeding off scrub vegetation.

Once the prairie chicken had an eastern cousin. The heath hen lived in the woods of New England and the adjoining north-eastern states, generally making its home where oak trees were to be found. Smaller than the prairie chicken, similar in colour but with pointed tuft-feathers at its neck instead of rounded ones, it fed on acorns and berries, wandering occasionally into open fields to eat clover leaves and grain. It made its nest in the oak woods, usually at the base of some large stump. The nest was no more than a hollow in the ground, lined with leaves and strands of grass, in which the heath hen laid a dozen or more creamy, green-tinged eggs.

When the Pilgrims landed, the heath hen was a fairly common bird, and the Puritan fathers enjoyed feasting on its tangy meat. They hunted the bird so frequently that they grew tired of it; servants in colonial times often complained about being served heath hen too often, and on one occasion went on strike to protest against getting it more than three times a week.

There were no game laws in early America, and the timing of the hunters was poor. They found it easiest to shoot the heath hen during the breeding season, when it stayed close to its nest. As a result, they not only killed off the adults but did away with the next generation as well. Not until much later did the concept of a 'closed season' take hold, in which the hunting of an animal is forbidden while the young are being reared. Today, 'to shoot a sitting duck' is proverbial for an unsportsmanlike act, but the Americans of three centuries ago saw nothing wrong in shooting down a heath hen while she sat on her nest.

The heavy hunting of the heath hen, especially wanton and short-sighted hunting of this sort, rapidly reduced the bird's population. Dogs and cats raided the heath hen's open, ground-level nests to feast on the eggs. The felling of the forests and the clearing of land for cultivation destroyed its nesting areas. Since New England was the first region of the United States to come under intensive agriculture, its forests were the first to go, and the heath hen was in trouble by the eighteenth century. As early as 1791 New York State passed a law prohibiting the hunting of this bird during the nesting season. But the law was poorly enforced. By 1870 there were no heath hens in New York State.

In New England, the bird had almost entirely vanished a few years earlier. Audubon, in 1830, had noted that its range was shrinking. Fifty years later, the shrinkage was all but total. The heath hen could be found only in one place: the wooded, sandy island of Martha's Vineyard, off the coast of Massachusetts. Protective laws were passed. Not many heath hens were left – about a hundred of them, in forty square miles – but in 1897 it was possible for one authority on birds to declare, 'the bird is in no present danger of extinction'.

No one was allowed to hunt the heath hen on Martha's Vineyard. Yet the population slowly dropped. A census in 1907 showed just seventy-seven heath hens left.

A public appeal for funds was launched to save the heath hen. Protective measures were increased and wardens watched over its nesting grounds. In the January 1912 issue of the *Bulletin of the New York Zoological Society*, Assistant Curator of Birds Lee S. Crandall reported, 'Now confined entirely to the island preserve on Martha's Vineyard . . . the cycles of the lives of these few individuals are guarded and watched as carefully as is [humanly] possible by wardens and scientific investigation.' In 1916, after eight years of such protection, the heath hen population on Martha's Vineyard showed a dramatic rise: from seventy-seven birds to nearly two thousand!

Heath Hens

But when a species is confined to one small area, even two thousand birds may not be enough to stave off extinction.

Fire raced across Martha's Vineyard in 1916. It was the nesting season for the heath hen, and many of the mother birds refused to leave their nests even when the flames came. After the fire was out saddened wardens inspected the island and found only 105 heath hens. Most of these were males.

Even so, the nesting birds raised eight to a dozen chicks at a time, and it might have been possible to bring the species back once more. But then came an unusually severe winter that killed many birds. After that, hawks invaded the island and did heavy damage. Then came an epidemic of disease. On 11 March 1932 the last heath hen died.

It was a bird that had never really stood a chance once the forests began to fall. The hunters who shot it down in the nesting season, the cats and dogs who stole its eggs, the farmers who turned its beloved woods into acres of farmland – all contributed to the end of the heath hen.

The *Vineyard Gazette,* a newspaper published on Martha's Vineyard, carried an obituary for the heath hen on 21 April 1933 written by the paper's owner, Arthur Beetle Hough. 'Now we know there are degrees even in death,' he wrote. 'All around us nature is full of casualties, but they do not interrupt the stream of life . . . But to the heath hen something more than death has happened, or, rather, a different kind of death. There is no survivor, there is no future, there is no life to be re-created in this form again. We are looking upon the uttermost finality which can be written, glimpsing the darkness which will not know another ray of light. We are in touch with the reality of extinction.'

The heath hen, the obituary declared, 'was a curious creature, an actor out of place, surviving beyond its appointed days'. It had long since ceased to have any economic importance, and had been preserved on Martha's Vineyard solely for sentiment's sake, as a reminder of the past. Making its home among the scrub oaks and ferns and gnarled pines of the small, quiet island, it 'lived a century beyond its time and then died, a single specimen making an end of the race, somewhere alone in the brush.

'The heath hen failed to adapt to changing conditions and fell a victim to the laws of natural selection. This is a curious thing, for until the white men took over the land, the heath hen had achieved an admirable adaptation, embodying such fine distinctions of nature that scientists appreciate their nicety and would like to understand them better. Even if you knew where a heath hen was, against a background of twigs and brush, you could not see it unless it moved. Failed to adapt! Why, no creature was ever more at home, more nicely adjusted to place and time than the heath hen on the Vineyard plains! The whole trouble lay in the fact that the heath hen was a bird man could kill, and so it had to die.'

In the American Museum of Natural History in New York, there is a realistic-looking display of a heath hen guarding a nest in which the first chicks have begun to hatch. There is a similar display in the Peabody Museum at Harvard. The stuffed birds are well mounted, and look as though they would like to leave their case and strut about the museum. They never will. Strutting heath hens are as unlikely now as dinosaurs parading on Fifth Avenue. 'The extinction of the heath hen,' Arthur Beetle Hough wrote in 1933, 'has taken away part of the magic of the Vineyard. This is the added loss of the island. There is a void in the April dawn, there is an expectancy unanswered, there is a tryst not kept.'

10

Back from Oblivion

'Extinct' is a terribly final word. But the world is large and has many dark corners in which the last survivors of a supposedly extinct species can lurk. Several times in this century we have had the happy surprise of removing from the rolls of the last species some creature that unexpectedly has turned up after having been missing for decades.

The quagga, the moa, the dodo, the passenger pigeon, the giant ground sloth, the great auk, Steller's sea cow, the heath hen, the aurochs – all these remain among the missing, despite the occasional rumour that tells of quaggas in South West Africa or sea cows off Siberia. But let us consider a few animals that might have been listed as extinct, but for lucky discoveries in recent years.

Notornis

The aquatic birds known as rails are found in many parts of the world. They live in marshes, hiding among the reeds and water plants, and when attacked they usually dive and swim away instead of taking to the air. More than half the known rails live confined to certain islands, and most of these have lost the use of their wings altogether.

New Zealand, that home of many flightless birds, had several marsh birds of this family that ornithologists were able to study in the nineteenth century. One, though, eluded all collectors. The Maoris spoke of it as the *moho*, a dark blue bird as big as a goose, which they had formerly hunted on the banks of lakes and rivers. The moho, said the Maoris, had now vanished from its North Island home.

In the 1840s, while the search for living moas was going on, scientists in New Zealand looked for the moho as well. No live ones were found, but in 1847 Walter Mantell, the government official whose hobby was fossil hunting, came upon the skull, breastbone, and several other bones of an unfamiliar bird. Mantell sent the bones to London with a note that the Maoris of North Island claimed these were the bones of the moho. The eminent palaeontologist Richard Owen, examining them, agreed that they had come from some member of the rail family. He gave it the name of *Notornis mantelli* in honour of its discoverer. Presumably *Notornis* was extinct.

In 1849 a party of seal hunters camped on South Island saw a remarkably attractive bird, and netted it. It was nearly two feet high, with iridescent indigo plumage on its neck, head, breast, and flanks, a scarlet beak, metallic purple feathers on its belly and thighs, olive green on its rump. Its legs and feet were bright red. Such a brilliantly coloured bird, they reasoned, must be valuable to some collector, so they killed it and carefully skinned it. By chance the skin came into the possession of Walter Mantell. He felt certain that it was the skin of a *Notornis*.

Mantell went to South Island and questioned the Maoris. They had never heard of the moho, but spoke of a bird called the *takahe*, which had blue plumage, red legs, and highly edible meat. Mantell guessed that the takahe of South Island and the moho of North Island were the same. The moho was almost certainly extinct, but apparently the takahe still survived.

In 1850 some Maoris brought Mantell the skin of a second takahe. They had seen its tracks on fresh snow, and had followed it with the aid of dogs. Mantell sent both skins to the British Museum to join the moho bones he had earlier collected. For many years the Notornis made no further news. Occasionally a Maori claimed to have seen one, or the tracks of one, but no specimens were taken. Ferdinand von Hochstetter, the Austrian ornithologist who came to New Zealand late in the nineteenth century to collect moas, also searched for *Notornis* and concluded that the two birds caught on South Island in 1849 and 1850 were unique. 'It appears to me,' he wrote, 'that this family of birds is now extinct.'

In December 1879 a man and his dog were out hunting

Notornis mantelli (Moho)

rabbits in the Province of Otago in southern South Island when the dog rushed into the underbrush and seized a large bird with a red bill, red legs, a glistening metallic blue neck, purple wings, and green shoulders. The dog's master promptly killed the bird and hung it up, planning to make a meal of it. But a friend wandered by and recognized it as *Notornis*, for which he knew museum directors would pay a good price. The bird was skinned and carefully prepared. Skin and skeleton went off to London, where they were auctioned before a group of museum representatives. The Dresden museum of Germany bought the third *Notornis* for £200.

Careful study at the museum showed that the takahe of South Island was somewhat different from the moho of North Island. So it was recognized as a separate species, called *Notornis hochstetteri* after the scientist who had sought so hard to find it. High prizes were offered for more specimens of either species of *Notornis*.

There were no takers. Some bones, two skins, a skull and one complete mounted bird and skeleton – that was all. By 1898 it seemed unlikely that a live *Notornis* would be seen again, though a partial skeleton was found on South Island in 1884 and a complete one in 1892. Then, in 1898, a dog once again caught a live takahe. Its master recognized the bird for what it was, and had it preserved complete, including the internal organs. It was bought by the museum of Otago University – the first *Notornis* to remain in the land of its discovery.

These infrequent sightings of the rare and beautiful *Notornis* provided renewed hope that live birds might one day be found. However, decades went by without any sign of one. Fifty years passed since the last *Notornis* sighting. Surely the bird must be extinct by now.

One man who disagreed was a New Zealand physician,

Dr Geoffrey B. Orbell. He owned a summer home at Lake Te Anau, South Island, not far from where the 1879 and 1898 birds had been caught. Hunters who ranged the area around the lake sometimes stopped to visit Dr Orbell and told him of glimpsing takahes in the thickly forested countryside. There was no reason to take these stories seriously; but in the spring of 1948, while on a hunting trip himself, Dr Orbell halted beside the shore of a remote mountain lake and saw large, unfamiliar footprints in the mud. An unknown birdcall sounded in the distance: two long, deep notes repeated twice. The lake, he knew, was known to the Maoris as *Kohakatakahea*, 'the nesting-place of the takahe'. Why not? This rarely visited lake, three thousand feet up in the heavily wooded mountains overlooking Lake Te Anau, might well be the home of the mysterious bird.

He made precise measurements of the prints and took them to Dr Robert A. Falla of the Dominion Museum,

Notornis hochstetteri (Takahe)

Wellington, New Zealand. Dr Falla agreed that they could be *Notornis* prints. Orbell said that he planned to lead a new expedition into the mountains; he would not catch or kill any of the birds if he found them, but merely hoped to observe them. He asked Dr Falla to have the little mountain lake declared a wildlife refuge if it proved to be the nesting grounds of the takahe.

On 20 November 1948 Dr Orbell and a friend returned to the lake, equipped with cameras, colour film, and fifty yards of fishing net. They hiked through dense woods laced with vines, making their way with difficulty over the damp, mossy ground. Less than twenty yards from the place where the tracks had been seen in April, they saw more tracks – and then a takahe! Orbell focused his movie camera as a second bird appeared and joined the first. When he had recorded them on film, he snared them in his net and tethered them to stakes at the lake shore so he could take still pictures. A third bird emerged, squawking loudly, and began to graze nearby. For more than an hour Dr Orbell studied and photographed the birds. Then he released them. As he left, he found a broken eggshell, bright yellow with brown speckles, and took it back with him.

A much larger scientific expedition, including Orbell and Dr Falla, came to the lake two months later. They counted the takahe population, studied its feeding and nesting habits, and measured its breeding area. Several colonies were discovered in the marshland, numbering fifty to a hundred birds. A dozen nests were found. At best each contained one egg, or a single newly hatched chick. Many eggs had been smashed and chicks killed by predatory animals.

Notornis hochstetteri, the takahe, was far from extinct, but its chances for survival did not look good. Only one small region still contained the bird, and that region was infested with hungry animals. The New Zealand government declared the little lake a nature preserve, and set aside a huge area of 62,000 acres around it as a protected area. The predatory animals, chiefly ermines, were trapped and taken away. Today the *Notornis* of South Island is holding its own and perhaps slowly gaining now that it is under protection. About three hundred birds are thought to exist, and new colonies have been discovered in the next valley south of what is now called Notornis Valley. Although it breeds slowly – many of its eggs are sterile and few chicks are hatched – it may survive if no enemies slip into its secluded forest home.

The Cahow

Bermuda is the largest of the Bermuda Islands, a group of coral outcroppings about six hundred miles east of South Carolina. They are named after Juan Bermudez, a sailor who was shipwrecked there in the sixteenth century. Several other ships were wrecked on the reefs of Bermuda in the years that followed, and when Sir George Somers and a party of colonists bound for Virginia were shipwrecked there in 1609, they liked the climate so well that they founded a permanent settlement.

A few years before Somers arrived, a Spaniard named Diego Ramirez anchored his galleon in a bay off one of the islands and sent a boat ashore to look for water. 'None was found,' he wrote. 'At dusk, such a shrieking and din filled the air that fear seized us. Only one variety of bird makes this noise, but the concerted yell is terrible and standing out from it were individual voices shouting *diselo! diselo!* [tell 'em! tell 'em!] One seaman said to me: "What is this devil trying to tell me? Out with it! Let's hear what it is!" I replied: "These are the devils reported to be about Bermuda." '

But the 'devils' turned out to be delicious birds. So many of them surrounded a man with a lantern that he could not keep clear of them, even with a club, and five hundred birds were killed and cooked. They 'proved to be very fat and fine', wrote Ramirez, and 'thereafter a capture was made every evening. The birds were so plentiful that 4,000 could be taken in a single bag. The men relished them enough to eat them all the time, and when we left we brought away more than 1,000 well dried and salted for the voyage.'

When the English settled Bermuda soon after, they also discovered this tasty sea bird. To them its call sounded like '*cahow! cahow!*' and that was what they named it. It was a large, web-footed flying bird somewhat like a petrel. William Strachey, a member of Sir George Somers' colony, wrote in 1610 that the cahows were never seen in summer, but 'in the darkest nights of November and December they would come forth, but not fly farre from home, and hovering in the ayre, and ovre the Sea, made a strange hollow and harsh howling'. He called them 'a good and well relished Fowle, fat and full as a partridge', and praised both their flesh and the taste of their eggs.

In 1691 Governor Nathaniel Butler of Bermuda wrote: 'For the cahowe ... is a night bird, and all the daye long lies in holes of the rocks, whence both themselves and their young are in great numbers extracted with ease, and prove (especially the young) so pleasing in a dish, as shamed I am to tell how many dosen of them have been devoured by some of our northern stomacks, even at one only meal.'

The cahow, unlike the dodo, the auk, and most of the other extinct birds we have discussed, was able to fly. But it was so trusting that it could be easily killed, and killed it was, by the thousands. The settlers devoured its young and its eggs. They brought pigs and rats to Bermuda, which had never had such animals before, and the pigs and rats invaded the cahow nests and feasted on the eggs. Man and his animals swept over the islands like a plague. By 1621 it was necessary to pass laws prohibiting the hunting of cahows, but Captain John Smith, writing about Bermuda and its birds in 1629, declared that the cahow was 'all gone'.

The cahow became a Bermuda legend. For nearly three centuries no one was quite sure what it had looked like, and it was confused with other species of petrels and even with the unrelated auks. In 1849 a dusky sea bird discovered on an islet in the Bermudas was said to be the long-lost cahow, but it was shown to be a different bird. Not until 1916, when cahow bones were found and identified in caves on the islands, did anyone have a clear idea of the cahow's appearance.

By then a live cahow had been sighted, though its discoverer was unaware of the fact.

Louis L. Mowbray, the director of the Bermuda Aquarium, had captured a bird on the islet of Gurnet Rock. He identified it as a New Zealand petrel and had it stuffed. Not for ten years did it occur to him to compare it with the skeleton of an 'extinct' cahow, and when he did, in 1916, he realized that he had unknowingly rediscovered the long-lost bird.

Finding another live specimen was a difficult chore. In 1935 a bird killed itself flying against the window of a Bermuda lighthouse, and the naturalist William Beebe, unable to identify it, sent it to Dr Robert Cushman Murphy of the American Museum of Natural History, New York. Dr Murphy wrote back in excitement that

Beebe had found the second known specimen of the cahow. The bird had been skinned and stuffed, and not thinking it was rare, Beebe had thrown the skeleton away. Hastily he went in search of it and found it – in a wicker fish trap. A friend had used the cahow meat for bait, but the bones were still on hand.

It was clear now that the cahow was not extinct. The coming of the Second World War forced Dr Murphy to postpone for many years a planned expedition to Bermuda in quest of the bird. In January 1951 he finally flew to Bermuda and explored a number of the smaller islets near the places where the cahows of 1906 and 1935 had been found. Within a few days, amazingly enough, the Murphy expedition came to a cactus-covered islet that had holes in the earth that could be the burrows of sea birds.

'Most of the tunnels,' Dr Murphy wrote, 'were both deep and crooked. Presently we located one in which an electric flashlight revealed a bird in the nest chamber. The entrance was at the rear of a rocky niche large enough to accommodate a man's head and shoulders . . . With a noose at the end of a bamboo we succeeded in hauling out the bird. There was a breathless moment before daylight showed it to be the longed-for but only half-anticipated cahow! Its egg could then be seen in the nest.

'Our almost unbelievable captive bit the hands that grasped it but only half-heartedly. Within a moment it became completely unresistant, allowing itself to be stroked, tickled, and passed from hand to hand. We banded and photographed it and jotted down hasty descriptions of its flesh colours, including the pink feet. When put on the ground, it scurried back to its egg.'

The ornithologists stood watch through the night. As darkness came, they 'began to see swift silhouettes of birds overhead and from time to time to hear single, soft *screepy* notes'. Then a group of cahows appeared. Rain started to fall, making things uncomfortable for the bird watchers on the little island, but they continued to monitor the activities of the cahows until midnight.

A hundred cahows were found altogether. The government of Bermuda promptly declared the islets on which they nested to be bird sanctuaries. Rats were eliminated from the islets as thoroughly as possible, and the nests were also protected against another enemy, the longtailed tropic bird, which was in the habit of entering a cahow tunnel to kill the fledgeling living there and make its own nest in its place. After three centuries of oblivion, the cahow of Bermuda has been removed from the roster of extinct birds. Just enough survived the feasts of the seventeenth century to keep the species alive.

Przewalski's Horse

The horse has had a complicated history. Its earliest known ancestor, *Eohippus*, was about the size of a medium-big dog; it had four toes on its front feet and three on the back. It was common in Europe and North America about 75 million years ago, but the European species became extinct. In North America, changing climate brought about changes in *Eohippus*, so that it increased in body size, became stronger and faster, and evolved a single strong hoof in place of its toes. The horse crossed the land bridge that once connected Alaska to Siberia and migrated into Asia and Europe. Eventually the horses of the Americas died out entirely, but those that had entered the Old World thrived.

Man tamed the wild horse of Europe and made it into

a beast of burden. Domestic horses came to look somewhat different from their wild cousins: their legs were more slender, their heads narrower. They were taller than wild horses, and had longer heads. Gradually the wild horse disappeared. The sculptured reliefs in Assyrian palaces show wild horses being hunted in the Near East 2,700 years ago. Roman writers distinguish between the domestic horse and the *hippagros*, or wild horse. Eventually the last wild horses of Europe were rounded up. Many were killed in hunts; others were mated with domestic horses, so that their special characteristics were lost. By A.D. 1000 or so, the true wild horse was gone from Europe.

In the sixteenth and seventeenth centuries there were reports of 'wild horse hunts' in the game preserves of German aristocrats. But these were horses of the domestic breed that had gone wild again. They did not have the physical traits of the original wild horse. So-called wild horses also appeared in the New World at this time, but they were domestic horses that had escaped from Spaniards and were running wild on the prairies.

Nor did the real wild horse – the horse of the ice ages – seem to exist in Asia, either. Everywhere in the world, apparently, this ancestral horse had been exterminated through hunting or extinguished through cross-breeding.

Then, in 1879, a Russian explorer named Nikolai Mikhailovitch Przewalski made a journey through the wild, almost unknown region called Dzungaria, in western Mongolia. He had spent many years exploring Siberia, Mongolia, Tibet, and Turkestan, and was familiar with the wildlife of the barren steppes that lay between Russia and China. He was in particular an expert on horses, and had studied the tough, speedy little steeds of the

Mongols, which he felt were closer in form to the ancient wild horse than any other breed. Because he knew these Mongol horses so well, Przewalski was startled one day to see a dozen horses of an entirely different breed gallop suddenly across his path and disappear.

In his one brief glimpse of these animals, Przewalski saw that they were yellowish brown in colour, with black manes and long black tails that nearly touched the ground. Their heads were unusually broad and their arched necks were thick and powerfully muscled. To Przewalski they seemed like exceptionally stocky ponies of an unfamiliar type.

He questioned the Mongols of the vicinity. They knew the horse well, and called it the *taki*; it was scarce and very shy, they said, and its meat was delicious. They regarded it as a slightly larger relative of their own breed of horses.

Przewalski's horse

Przewalski set out on the trail of the taki. A few days later he saw another band of them and got a better look as they sped past him. They had small ears, white bellies, dark legs marked with bars below the knees, and a dark stripe down their backs. He wrote a detailed description of this short-legged, big-headed, rather ungainly-looking horse and sent it to a zoologist friend in Russia, J.S. Polyakov. Polyakov wrote back to say that Przewalski had undoubtedly discovered the supposedly extinct wild horse of the glacial era.

The explorer himself disagreed. As an expert on all breeds of horses, he thought that this little yellowish-brown Mongolian animal was a relative of the onager, or, hemionus, a type of horse still found in other parts of Asia. Przewalski could not believe that such a stocky, coarse-looking beast could be ancestral to the slender, handsome, graceful horses he had admired all his life.

However, the evidence of the cave paintings of pre-historic Europe showed that Polyakov was right. Twenty thousand years ago and more, Cro-Magnon man and other artistically inclined hunters of the ice ages had depicted in realistic guise the animals of their era. The horses of the cave paintings were unmistakably of the same type as Przewalski's horse. The herd in Dzungaria represented the last examples of this ancient breed, long extinct everywhere else in the world.

There was a double resurrection of Przewalski's horse. The Mongols, as Przewalski had discovered, enjoyed the meat of this animal, and, since they had no need of it for transportation, killed it for food whenever they could. It was only a matter of luck that Przewalski had found the horses when he had, for there were only about a hundred left, and in another generation they would surely have been wiped out.

A few foals were captured and were nursed by domestic Mongolian mares. They were purchased by European collectors, who bred them in captivity. The Duke of Bedford, who had saved the European bison from extinction almost single-handedly by rearing them on his large estate, acquired a few. A Russian agriculturist, Friedrich Falz-Fein, purchased some. So did the Hamburg zoo. These collectors sold breeding pairs to various zoos. By 1955, when about 90 Przewalski's horses were known in captivity, zoologists reported that the species was extinct in the wild. It had been saved by the devoted scientists who had nurtured it in Europe.

The obituary turned out to be slightly premature. A Russian exploring party in that same year of 1955 found a few wild Przewalski's horses in Mongolia, near two mountain ranges. They estimated that the wild herds numbered about forty members. The government of Mongolia prohibited any further hunting of the animals, and collected some to breed. Today the Prague Zoological Gardens, Czechoslovakia, is raising a stock of these horses which will eventually be turned loose in Mongolia to replenish the wild herds.

The prehistoric wild horse, then, was written off too quickly as extinct. The survival of this mammal in a remote part of Asia has encouraged optimists to think that other large animals such as the quagga may yet similarly come to light, but there seems to be small hope of that.

The Ivory-Billed Woodpecker

One of the most beautiful of all American birds, the ivory-billed woodpecker, was a sight available only to those willing to pursue it to its haunts in the primeval forest. John James Audubon saw this largest of wood-peckers when it still could be found, more than 130 years ago, in the woods of the Mississippi Valley and the southern Atlantic states.

'I have visited the favourite resort of the Ivory-Billed Woodpecker,' Audubon wrote in 1825, 'those deep morasses overshadowed by millions of gigantic, dark, moss-covered cypresses which seem to admonish intruding man to pause and reflect on the many difficulties ahead. If he persists in venturing farther into these almost inaccessible recesses, he must follow for miles a tangle of massive trunks of fallen, decaying trees, huge projecting branches, and thousands of creeping and twining plants of numberless species! ... Would that I could give you an idea of the sultry, pestiferous atmosphere that nearly suffocates the intruder during the noon-day heat of the dog-days in those gloomy and horrible swamps!'

At the end of the quest, though, was a spectacular bird with deep blue-black feathers marked with white patches, topped by a blazing red crest. Its three-inch-long ivory-coloured bill was as effective as a hatchet for ripping the bark from dead trees, revealing the beetles and grubs beneath. 'I have seen it detach pieces of bark seven or eight inches long with a single blow of its powerful bill,' wrote Audubon. 'By beginning at the top branch of a dead tree, it will tear off the bark for twenty or thirty feet in a few hours, leaping downwards with its body in an upward position. All the while it tosses its head to right and left, or leans it against the bark to detect the spot where the grubs are concealed. Immediately afterwards it renews its blows with fresh vigour, sounding its loud notes as if highly delighted.'

These clear, high, resonant cries of the ivory-billed

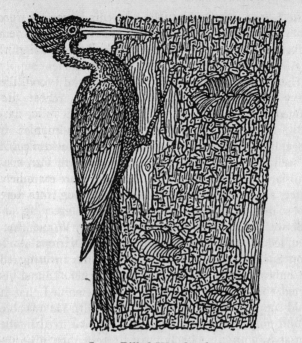

Ivory-Billed Woodpecker

woodpecker could be heard more than half a mile away. That allowed Indians to find and kill the birds. They valued its red crest as an ornament for their war costumes, and also prized its bill. 'I have seen entire belts of Indian chiefs closely ornamented with the tufts and bills of this species,' said Audubon, 'and have observed that a great value is frequently put upon them.'

The Indian hunters helped to reduce the numbers of these birds. Far more serious, though, was the felling of the southern forests. The ivory-billed woodpecker would live only in the highest trees of a virgin forest, and when those forests were logged, their breeding grounds were taken away. Since each nesting pair of ivory-billed woodpeckers insisted on having at least six square miles of virgin forest to itself, in order to find a sufficient supply of the insects that were the ivory-bill's only food, the heavy logging of the nineteenth century rapidly destroyed its habitat.

By 1900 it was gone from the northern part of its range. Fifteen years later, ivory-billed woodpeckers could be seen only in the swamp forests of South Carolina, Louisiana, and Florida. Even there they were extremely scarce, and more than a hundred of the survivors were shot so museums might have stuffed specimens.

Between 1947 and 1950 James Tanner, an ornithologist, led a study group sponsored by the National Audubon Society and Cornell University that investigated the habitat of the ivory-billed woodpecker. Tanner reported that so little unspoiled forest remained that it could support at best twenty-five ivory-bills. He was able to find only five in three years. These five lived in the Tensas Swamp, a privately owned forest tract in northeastern Louisiana.

An attempt was made to purchase the swamp as a sanctuary, but nothing came of it, and the loggers moved in to chop down many of the tallest trees. In 1951 only two ivory-bills could be found there. Both of them were females.

Later that year, Roger Tory Peterson, another ornithologist, entered the area to search for the birds. He found only two females also, probably the same two that had been seen earlier. 'We followed the big woodpeckers for nearly an hour before we lost them,' he wrote. 'As mated ivory-bills accompany each other throughout the year, it could be surmised that there were no males about and these females were forced to resort to their own sex for companionship.'

Two female birds could not continue the species. The pair was sighted now and then during 1952 but it was assumed that when they died, the ivory-bill would be extinct. After a while even those two could no longer be located.

Just as scientists were beginning to class it with the dodo and the auk, the ivory-billed woodpecker unexpectedly reappeared in Florida after several years without sightings. Six birds were seen in 1960. A secret and guarded reservation covering a thousand acres has been set aside in the hope that these few woodpeckers will be able to re-establish the species. For the time being, this bird must come off the list of extinct creatures, but the outlook for its continued survival is not very good.

I I

Saved at the Brink

There have always been a few people who have tried to save unique and irreplaceable animals from disappearance. Sometimes their voices have gone unheard, as with Jakovlev, who attempted to have Steller's sea cow placed under protection in 1755. Sometimes their efforts have been in vain, as in the case of those who worked to preserve the heath hen, the quagga, and the passenger pigeon. And sometimes they have succeeded in pulling a species back from the brink of extinction. The European and American bison, Przewalski's horse, the cahow, *Notornis,* and the ivory-billed woodpecker are examples of animals whose last survivors have come under protection – often, as we have seen, after the species was thought to be extinct.

In recent years several other heroic rescue attempts have met with good luck – so far. That any of the animals of this chapter still can be seen in zoos around the world is entirely the doing of individuals who worked to spare them from the fate of the moa, the aurochs, and the dodo.

Père David's Deer

In 1861, when he was twenty-five years old, a French missionary named Armand David went to China. Père

David's father, a physician, had wanted his son to study medicine as well, and had encouraged him to learn anatomy, zoology, and botany. Young Armand, though he chose the priesthood as his vocation, received a sound and thorough grounding in natural history.

During the eleven years he spent in China, Père David undertook some half-dozen large-scale scientific expeditions into distant provinces. He discovered a great many plants unknown to science, and also a host of insects and mammals, specimens of which he shipped to museums and zoological gardens in France. One of his discoveries was the giant panda, a rare animal that looks like a black-and-white bear, but which is actually a relative of the racoon. Today only about fifty giant pandas are thought to exist in the bamboo forests of China's Szechuan Province, plus a few kept in zoos, so this attractive and interesting animal is probably close to extinction. Père David's name, though, is much more closely associated with an unusual species of deer that he found in the year 1865.

Père David did not find the deer that bears his name on one of his expeditions. He discovered it several miles south of Peking, in the Nan Hai-tzu Imperial Park, a royal game preserve. This park, established in the fourteenth century, was surrounded by a high wall forty-five miles in length, and it was forbidden to enter or even to peep over the wall. Somehow Père David learned that 'sacred animals' lived in the park.

Curiosity triumphed over virtue. The missionary slipped a small bribe to the park's Mongolian guards and was allowed to climb over the wall. Within, he found a large head – some 120 head – of a strange deer with broad spreading hoofs, a long shaggy tail, and big antlers. They looked something like reindeer, except that they carried their heads close to the ground as a bison might do.

Père David asked some questions. He learned that the deer were called *sse-pu-hsiang*, which meant 'not deer, not ox, not goat, not donkey'. This odd name seemingly was coined because the animal had hoofs something like a goat's, a tail as long as a cow's ending in coarse hair like a horse's, and the general appearance of a deer – yet was not really any of these four. The guards said that the sse-pu-hsiang had lived in the imperial park as long as anyone could remember, but was found nowhere else, either wild or in captivity.

At Père David's request, the French ambassador in Peking asked the Chinese authorities for one of the deer. The request was refused. But in January 1866 Père David quietly obtained two complete skins, probably by bribing the park guards once more, and shipped them to France. 'I have been trying for a long time to obtain a specimen of this interesting member of the deer family that is still unknown to science,' he wrote in an accompanying letter. Soon after, the Chinese government relented and decided to bestow three of the deer on the French. The animals died on the voyage to Europe, though.

The zoologist Alphonse Milne-Edwards, a friend of Père David's, studied the two skins and the three dead deer in Paris and published the first scientific paper on the animal. He gave it the scientific name *Elaphurus davidianus*, making it a new species of the deer family. Through an error, Milne-Edwards reported that the animal was known in China as the *mi-lu*. This was really the name of another deer found in Manchuria and Japan. 'But 'mi-lu' was easier to pronounce than 'sse-pu-hsiang', and Père David's deer is still referred to as the mi-lu by European zoologists a century later.

When word got out that China had given three specimens of this rare deer to France, all the other European nations demanded some as well. In 1869 the London Zoo received two live ones, and shortly after the German diplomats in China were able to obtain a few. In the following twenty years, more Père David's deer found their way to European zoos. They bred readily in captivity. With more than a hundred of the deer still in China, and a dozen or so in Europe, the species seemed in no danger.

The Duke of Bedford, that wealthy and enlightened collector of rare animals, decided to have his own herd of Père David's deer. He could not get any from China, but he began to buy the surplus offspring born in the zoos of

Père David's deer

Europe. Within a few years he had assembled a herd of eighteen young deer. They found the lakes of the Duke's estate much to their liking, and the English weather was not very different from that of Peking. Like the swamp dwellers they once had been, they spent most of their time wading in search of water plants. In this semi-wild condition they surprised zoologists by shedding their antlers twice a year, something no other kind of deer does.

In 1895 a catastrophic flood swept through the country south of Peking. The old and crumbling wall of the imperial game preserve was breached. Many of the animals were drowned by the rampaging waters. Others escaped, including most of the deer. They fled into the countryside and were promptly killed and eaten by hungry peasants. The keepers of the park could round up only about thirty of Père David's deer.

Even these survivors were not spared. Five years later, an anti-European uprising called the Boxer Rebellion broke out in China. The rebels attacked the districts where European missionaries and businessmen lived, burning their homes and killing many of them. To protect their interests, the nations of Europe sent a joint army into China, under command of a German general. The European soldiers, after they had crushed the rebellion, broke into the imperial game preserve and proceeded to turn Père David's deer into venison. Only one deer, a female, survived. She died of old age in 1920.

That eliminated the Chinese herd – and, but for the chance discovery of the deer by Père David in 1865, the species would have been extinct. Because he had called the animal to the attention of the zoo-keepers of Europe, a few of the deer had been exported from China before the double disasters of the flood and the rebellion.

But, strangely, all of the Père David's deer in the European zoos were dead by 1920.

They had reproduced rapidly at first. Then the mounting demand for the deer had caused the zoos to break up their herds, selling the 'extra' animals and keeping only one breeding pair. However, the deer did not do well when kept in isolated pairs. Apparently they could thrive only as a herd. One by one, the zoo deer died off, and fewer offspring were born each year, until during the First World War the last animals were dead.

The Duke of Bedford still had his herd, though. Quietly, without calling attention to his deer, he had watched his original eighteen deer multiply until by 1914 he had close to ninety. Half of these died during the war from hunger, because the Duke could not obtain a sufficient supply of winter fodder for them. Even so, in 1920, when all other Pére David's deer were gone, he proudly announced that he had a breeding stock of fifty head.

Without reducing the numbers of his herd severely, the Duke began to sell a few of his deer to the eager zoos. A new breeding herd was established at the London Zoo, and at various other zoos throughout Europe. The Bronx Zoo in New York obtained a pair, and in 1950 the birth of the first Père David's deer on American soil was recorded. Long extinct in the wild, preserved by good fortune in an emperor's private park, Père David's deer exists today solely through the curiosity of a French priest and the devotion of an English duke. Woburn Abbey, the Duke of Bedford's estate, now has hundreds of Père David's deer in its herd, and there are large, increasing herds in zoos in London, New York, and elsewhere.

The Trumpeter Swan

The magnificent swan, found only in North America, is the world's largest waterfowl. It stands four feet high, has a wingspread of seven or eight feet, and weighs twenty to thirty pounds. Its bill is jet black, distinguishing it from other species of swans, and its voice, a great booming bellow, gives it its name.

Once the trumpeters were abundant from the Arctic Ocean to Missouri, from the western prairies as far east as Wisconsin and Indiana. They were seen on lakes and ponds along the Atlantic coast in winter, and large flocks of them nested in Chesapeake Bay. It was a stirring sight when a V-shaped formation of these superb birds moved across the sky.

The big white birds made an easy target, though. Their meat provided a feast fit for a king – how splendid to dine on roast swan! – and their fluffy feathers made good pillow stuffing. Towards the end of the eighteenth century the swans were nearly exterminated in the eastern part of their range, although Audubon saw flocks of several hundred as late as the 1820s. He reported that quantities of the swans had been shot along the Gulf Coast and sold in the markets of New Orleans.

As the slaughter went on, the trumpeter retreated to inaccessible northern regions in Oregon, Washington, and Canada. They were pursued even there. The Hudson's Bay Company, the great Canadian trading establishment, recorded selling seventeen thousand swans for their feathers between 1853 and 1857. Most of these were trumpeters. After 1877, so few of the birds remained that hunting them became unprofitable. Their numbers continued to decline until by 1900 they were thought to be nearly extinct, perhaps completely gone.

About twenty years later, a few breeding pairs appeared in Yellowstone National Park. These were protected, of course. A swan census showed seventy-three trumpeters in 1935. From bitter experience conservationists knew how risky it was to depend on a single colony of a rare species, and so in 1938 the United States Government began transplanting some of the Yellowstone swans to other parks. Several young swans were placed in the marshes of the National Elk Refuge in Wyoming. They thrived, and attracted other swans still living in the wild, forming a new colony. The following year some

Trumpeter Swan

trumpeters were taken to the Malheur Refuge in Oregon, and they, too, nested and began to breed. Other flocks were established at the Ruby Lake Refuge in Nevada, the Delta Waterfowl Research Station in Manitoba, and Red Rocks Lake in Montana.

Since the trumpeters did not nest and begin to hatch young swans until they were about five years old, the growth of these flocks was slow. But by 1941 there were 211 birds, and 763 were counted in 1958 – a tenfold growth in twenty-three years. In 1960, trumpeters were moved east of the Rocky Mountains for the first time since they had been killed off there in the nineteenth century, and three years later two pairs of trumpeter swans in the Lacreek National Wildlife Refuge in South Dakota made nests and produced broods of healthy cygnets.

The trumpeter swan is in no danger of extinction today. More than fifteen hundred exist in bird sanctuaries in the United States and Canada, protected by law and guarded against those who still would slay any wild creature, no matter how beautiful or how rare.

The Nene

Most species of geese live in cool climates and stay close to water. The nene (pronounced *nay-nay*), or Hawaiian goose, makes its home on the dry lava beds of tropical volcanoes. Perhaps once it was a migratory bird of the north, like its cousins, but thousands of years ago the nene reached Hawaii, found that it liked the special conditions of the volcanic islands, and remained.

Even though its habitat was an unusual one – the cinders and ash and twisted tinkling blackness of a lava bed, desert-dry and covered with gnarled shrubs – the nene thrived. At one time more than twenty-five thousand of them lived on the islands of Maui and Hawaii.

Then came man.

The Hawaiian Islands were settled by Polynesians about AD 500. These brown-skinned people long lived in isolation, as did their relatives, the Maoris of New Zealand. They hunted the birds of the island for food and their ornamental plumage. Like most island groups cut off from the rest of the world, Hawaii had evolved a number of unusual birds that are found nowhere else. Nearly two dozen of these became extinct as a result of such hunting.

The nene, though, did not arouse much interest in the natives. This upright-standing goose, two feet high, was dreary in colour – dark brown above, light brown below, with black tail, wings, and bill. Its dull plumage had no ornamental value. The meat was good, but so was the meat of other birds. Some of the islanders kept the nene as a pet.

Captain Cook discovered Hawaii for Europe in 1778 – and lost his life there. Before long, white men were coming to the lovely islands in great numbers. They brought with them their religions, their political ideas, and their diseases. The natives suffered severely, their population dropping from 300,000 around 1770 to 50,000 a century later. The wildlife of the islands suffered also.

To the newcomers, the nene was a great delicacy. The geese were so tame that hunters entering the lava fields were able to kill hundreds of them in a few hours' time. The birds were eaten locally, but also were salted and packed in barrels to be sold to passing whaling vessels. Clipper ships took cargoes of nene to California as food for the forty-niners. Very quickly the nene began to disappear.

Game laws gave the nene small protection. The nene season lasted four and a half months, and each hunter was allowed to kill six birds a day. By 1902, naturalists were warning that the bird would soon be extinct if the hunts continued, but not until 1911 was the nene finally put under protection. By that time it was unnecessary to do so; less than a hundred wild nene existed, and hunters found it too much bother to go after them.

In 1918 a rancher named Herbert C. Shipman decided to try to save the nene from extinction. Shipman lived near the coastal town of Hilo on the island of Hawaii, known as 'the big island' to Hawaiians. As a boy he had seen the wild geese flying over the rugged lava-covered slopes around the Mauna Loa volcano. Flocks of nene were no longer seen in the air.

Shipman obtained a pair of the geese and began to breed them. In a few years he had a small flock of tame nene. Since the wild nene was nearly extinct, Shipman contributed a few of his birds to the new Mokapu Game Farm on the island of Oahu in 1927. The game farm was able to raise its own flock of nene, and sent pairs of them to the islands of Kauai, Molokai, and Lanai. But the nene had never lived in the wild state on those islands. It seemed to thrive only in the eerie, forlorn wasteland of a lava bed, and the conditions for its successful rearing existed only on the islands of Maui and Hawaii. The birds sent to the other islands did not form breeding colonies. By the 1930s, they all were dead, leaving only the Shipman flock. As for the wild nene, it was extinct on Maui and down to about a dozen birds on the island of Hawaii.

Shipman's birds did well, and his flock grew until there were nearly fifty nene in it. One year eight fully grown birds flew away; another year five disappeared. They were believed to have escaped to the lava beds of Mauna Loa, forty miles away, to take up life in the wild again. In April 1946 there were forty-three birds in the Shipman flock when a great tsunami, or 'tidal wave', struck. A wall of water smashed against the Shipman estate. Only eleven nene escaped drowning.

These birds were the only surviving nene in captivity. They and perhaps two or three dozen wild birds stood between the Hawaiian goose and extinction. Mr Shipman, taking no further chances, moved his remaining birds inland to a ranch near the crater of Kilauea, an inactive volcano.

The Hawaiian government had now become concerned with the plight of the nene. In 1948 it appropriated $6,000, nearly £2,200, for a breeding programme designed to rear nene in captivity and release them in protected parks on Maui and Hawaii. Mr Shipman made four of his birds available for the project. A fifth was donated by the Honolulu Zoo, and a sixth was a wild bird that had been caught by a hunter's dog.

Thanks to Herbert Shipman's years of studying this bird, a great deal had been learned about how to raise it in captivity, and the breeding programme was a success. A government-owned site in the middle of the island of Hawaii became a nene farm. Normally each bird laid three to five eggs a year, but the keepers of this farm at Pohakuloa discovered the trick of taking a nene's eggs away from her soon after they were laid and giving them to another bird to hatch. The first bird would then lay several more eggs. These, too, would be taken away, and the nene would produce a third clutch of eggs, which she would be permitted to hatch herself. This made the nene flock vastly more productive than it ordinarily would have been. So that few female nenes would be 'wasted' sitting on eggs when they could be laying new ones, the keepers trained ordinary hens to hatch nene eggs. Nene eggs are about three times as big as hen's eggs, so the barnyard fowl were trained by sitting them on large wooden eggs until they were willing to sit on the genuine variety.

The nene campaign became an international one in 1949 when the International Union for the Protection of

Nature, an organization sponsored by the United Nations, listed the nene as one of the world's thirteen most threatened bird species. The Wildfowl Trust, a British conservationist group, became interested in raising nene in Britain. There are no lava beds in Britain, but the curator of the Wildfowl Trust came to Pohakuloa and spent a season studying ways of raising nene in other habitats. He took two nene back to Britain with him in

Nene

1950, thinking that he had a breeding pair. A slight mistake had been made, though – both birds turned out to be female! Pohakuloa contributed an authentic gander the following year, and in 1952 nine healthy nene chicks were born in England.

Since then, more than two hundred nene have been reared by the Wildfowl Trust and have been distributed to game breeders in five other European countries. In 1958 a pair of nene was sent to a farm in Litchfield, Connecticut, and by the end of 1965 some twenty-five nene had been reared there.

The world population of nene thus grew to more than five hundred birds. In 1948, when the project had begun, thirteen nene existed in captivity and perhaps thirty more in the wild. More than three hundred nene bred in captivity have been released to join their wild kindred on Maui and Hawaii. Interestingly, ninety-three of these nene were sent back from Britain by the wildfowl Trust and seven were raised in Connecticut – so the cycle of nene rescue came all the way around when foreign-bred birds were sent home to their ancestral islands.

The nene has established itself once again in Hawaii – the first time that the wild population of a rare bird has been replenished with birds bred in captivity. It is now the official state bird of Hawaii, and its survival is a matter of pride to every islander.

There are several wild flocks. On Hawaii, the birds inhabit a 600-square-mile region of jagged lava country between the two great volcanoes Mauna Loa and Mauna Kea. Nearly 250 nene live there. More than 100 dwell on the neighbouring island of Maui in a twenty-square-mile zone around the dormant volcano Haleakala. The nene make their nests in hot, dry country where the twisted, tortured old lava flows provide an eerie landscape that seems to belong to another planet. Yet enough grasses and herbs grow in the volcanic ash to keep the birds well fed. Their enemies – the mongoose, the wild dog, wildcat, and wild pig – have difficulty reaching them there. Occasionally the Hawaiian hawk swoops down to seize one of the geese, but this hawk is itself a rare bird, close to extinction, and its raids are infrequent.

The nesting season for nene runs from October to March. Pairs of the birds seek out meadows on the higher slopes to make their nests. The young birds, born at the beginning of the year, are flightless until May. Each summer, new groups of domestic-bred nene are released in the parks and fly off to join the others.

It is too early to say that the nene has been saved from extinction for ever. But there are more nene in the world each year than there were the year before, and this goose of the lava fields no longer stands in immediate danger.

12

On Their Way Out

Not all vanishing species can be saved the way the nene, the trumpeter swan, and Père David's deer have been saved. Some, because of their way of life, may not be reared in captivity by conservationists. Others exist in such small numbers that even the most tender care can do little to stave off the inevitable end. And others, though under protection, remain vulnerable to enemies who are likely to bring about their extinction sooner or later.

The ferocious tiger is among the doomed in many parts of the world, for example. A number of local varieties of tiger have been reduced to extremely low numbers. Rarest of all is the Bali tiger. Only three or four still exist, on the western tip of this Indonesian island. Nearby Java's sub-species of tiger has only nine living representatives. The Caspian tiger of Iran, Afghanistan, and south-eastern Russia has less than fifty left. Half a dozen other big cats likewise stand just a few rifle shots away from oblivion.

In Florida's Everglades, a large hawk-like bird known as the Everglade kite is near its end. Five males and four females are definitely known to be alive in a wildlife refuge, and two or three others are thought to live just outside the sanctuary. This bird feeds only on a single

California Condor

species of large water snail which has grown quite rare. During the nesting season, the wildlife refuge where the kites live is closed to visitors so that the birds will not be disturbed, but their continued survival now appears doubtful.

The California condor, a giant bird of the far west, is restricted to the coast of southern California. This great hunting bird, which flies as high as twenty thousand feet and can soar for an hour without flapping its wings, numbers only forty to fifty today. Occasionally one is killed by some local hunter.

The condors are extremely sensitive to disturbance, abandoning their nests when anyone approaches, even leaving eggs or chicks behind. Civilization comes closer to the last nesting grounds of this condor every year. It now lives only in a remote refuge, under strong protection, but there is no great optimism expressed for its continued existence.

Many other endangered animals are near the point of no return. These are a few that may be among tomorrow's extinctions.

The Oryx

There are many species of antelope, but none is more beautiful than the Arabian oryx. This handsome cream-coloured desert animal has two long, sharp horns, so straight that seen from the side it appears that the oryx has but a single horn. It is thought that the ancient legend of the mythical unicorn arose when travellers saw distant oryxes from the side.

The oryx is a beast of formidable endurance. It withstands extreme desert temperatures that range from 140 degrees to the freezing point. Its speed is unusually great.

It can go for many days without water. The desert tribes-men of the Near East admire it for its strength and toughness. They believe that the man who kills an oryx will inherit its courage and vigour.

For centuries it has been a point of pride among these people to go out into the desert and prove manhood by slaying an oryx. So relentlessly has the oryx been hunted that it has disappeared from most of the Near East. In the early eighteenth century it was already regarded as a rarity, and the Shah of Persia preserved a small herd of them in his private park as curiosities. Once widespread in Syria, Iraq, and Arabia, the oryx was wiped out every-where by the beginning of the twentieth century except in the part of Arabia known as *Rub al-Khali*, 'the empty quarter'.

It is a real test of manhood to go hunting in Rub al-Khali. It is one of the world's most inhospitable deserts, where the sun glares down like a giant eye and the tem-perature rarely gets below 120 degrees in daytime. About a hundred oryxes inhabited this desert at the turn of the century – the world's last herd. Arab sheikhs, mounted on camels, going forth to demonstrate their virility, tracked these survivors. The contest was nearly an equal one. The chase was gruelling, the oryxes hard to find and quick to flee. Few kills were made.

After the Second World War, the wealthy Arabian po-tentates found an easier way of attaining the oryx's legendary qualities of strength and endurance. Dis-daining the risks of the lonely camel treks, they set out in caravans of jeeps, armed with machine guns. Some three hundred men at a time would enter the desert, roaring over the dunes in their speedy vehicles. The cars swept down on the oryx herd and a deadly hail of bullets cut the panicking animals down as they tried to escape.

After the last of these massacres, it seemed for a while as though the efficient sportsmen had succeeded in destroying all of the world's remaining oryxes. Wildlife conservationists exploring Rub al-Khali could locate only two survivors. One died of bullet wounds soon after it was found. The other, a female, was taken to the London Zoo.

It turned out that the oryx was not quite extinct. About two dozen of the animals still lived in the desert. In addition, King Saud of Saudi Arabia owned a small herd that was being bred to supply royal hunts. The Fauna Preservation Society, an English conservationist group, realized that a few more machine-gun safaris would end the species and rob mankind of one of its most attractive animals. Funds were raised to collect a herd of oryxes that could be reared in captivity.

Major Ian Grimwood, then the chief game warden of Kenya, led a seven-man expedition into the Arabian desert in 1962. Using spotter planes, they covered six thousand miles of emptiness and located four oryxes. These were caught with great difficulty – Major Grimwood suffered two broken ribs during the chase – and were taken to a special camp in Kenya. One of the four died after its capture, and a high-calibre bullet was discovered in its leg; it was a delayed victim of an Arab hunting party.

After several months the three healthy oryxes were shipped to Phoenix, Arizona. The dry climate of Arizona is similar to that of Arabia, and it was hoped that the animals would be comfortable there. The Phoenix Zoo set aside special quarters for the oryxes. They were joined shortly by the female that had been in the London Zoo, and by a fifth oryx presented by the Sultan of Kuwait, an Arabian ruler.

These five animals became the nucleus of what was called 'the World Herd' of oryxes. In October 1963 an oryx calf was born in the zoo. It was 16 inches tall, with long ears, bright brown eyes, and a short fuzzy tail, and it represented the first real hope that the oryx could be saved.

By that time the World Herd had grown considerably in size. The World Wildlife Fund, another con-

Oryx

servationist organization, had sponsored a second search for wild oryxes in April 1963. None were located in the desert, but King Saud was persuaded to part with four animals from the stock on his private game farm. Two males and two females – one of them pregnant – were shipped from Saudi Arabia to Italy, where they remained in quarantine for sixty days. In July they were flown to New York and spent some more time at a government quarantine station in New Jersey, where they were checked for possible diseases. Finally they were cleared and sent to Phoenix.

Two more oryx calves were born soon after the first. By the end of 1963 the Phoenix herd numbered twelve. The animals are doing well and their numbers will probably increase. As for the wild oryx, nobody knows how many survive, but there may be no more than a dozen. The next brave band of jeep-mounted hunters may account for those. One day the Phoenix oryxes may be the only ones left, and a single herd is but a fragile bulwark against total extinction.

The Whooping Crane

Each autumn a tense drama takes place at the Aransas National Wildlife Refuge near San Antonio, Texas, on the Gulf Coast. Anxious members of the refuge staff search the salt flats of the shoreline every October for signs of great white birds with black-tipped wings, long black legs, and bright patches of bare red skin on their heads. These are the whooping cranes. Less than fifty are left in the world, and they come to Aransas to spend the winter.

What makes the arrival of the whoopers so tense is the fact that they must fly 2,500 miles from their nesting grounds in Canada's North-west Territories. Down over Canada they come, through the Dakotas, Nebraska, Kansas, Oklahoma, Texas. They are at the mercy of any hunter along the way who cares to shoot at them. Of course, they are protected by law, but that does not always deter the unscrupulous killer who wishes to test his aim against the majestic bird high overhead. And some hunters mistake the whoopers for the sandhill crane. It is legal to shoot at sandhills; nothing can be done to remedy the mistake if the dead bird turns out to be a whooper.

So the keepers of the Aransas sanctuary wait in hope and fear as the whoopers make their annual southward migration. They know the older birds by sight, and welcome them back like good friends. They grieve when one of the familiar whoopers fails to appear. They rejoice when a pair of cranes arrives with a youngster born during the summer. They count the whoopers and publish the totals, hoping to be able to show a few more whoopers this year than the year before.

In the spring the drama begins again. It is nesting time, and the cranes leave Texas for the return journey to Canada. They reach the north woods in April – those that make it safely – and sound their loud bugle-like whooping cries to announce their return. They build their nests, lay their eggs, hatch the young whoopers and teach them to fly, getting them ready for the long autumn flight that awaits them.

It seems impossible that the birds can survive the hazards of the long migration. There are so few of them, and so many rifles. Yet their numbers are gradually increasing. In 1938, the lone flock consisted of just 18 birds. By 1956 there were twenty-eight, and two years later thirty-two birds were counted, twenty-three of them adults and nine young born that year. (A tenth young crane got lost coming south and landed safely in Missouri, the first time a whooper had been seen there since 1913. It flew north in the spring and joined the others.) Some years the population went up by one or two, some years it dipped. The count in 1961 showed forty-six birds, but two years later there were only forty; in 1966 the total was forty-four. In addition, there are five in captivity. The Audubon Park Zoo, New Orleans, had a pair named Crip and Josephine, who produced two chicks in 1957 and a third in 1958. Josephine, who was more than twenty-five years old, died of excitement at the zoo during a hurricane in 1965. The other captive crane is Rosey, at the San Antonio zoo in Texas.

Whooping cranes were never common birds. Probably they numbered no more than two or three thousand at best, even before man came to the New World. The first record of one comes from Mark Catesby, the English naturalist, who bought the skin of a whooper from an Indian of the Carolinas in 1722. Samuel Hearne, who explored northern Canada between 1769 and 1772, wrote, 'They are generally seen only in pairs, and that not very often.' In 1805, Lewis and Clark saw a few migrating whoopers in the north-west, but even Audubon, that indefatigable seeker of rare birds, saw the crane only once.

Originally the whoopers nested in the prairie lands of North Dakota, Minnesota, Illinois, and Iowa. But as settlers transformed wilderness into farmland, the whoopers had to spend their summers ever farther to the north. The last nesting in the United States was recorded in 1894. Even Canada offered them little true wilderness, so that they were forced to nest at the edge of the Arctic. About a thousand birds still remained at the beginning of this century, but hunters showed little mercy, killing 30 per cent of the entire population in one ten-year period. By 1922 the whooping crane was so rare that its extinction was considered a matter of a few more years. The long migratory flights were too perilous, although the birds were safe once they reached their nesting grounds. No one even knew where those nesting grounds were.

The winter nesting grounds at the Aransas sanctuary were discovered in 1937. It was lucky that the cranes had chosen a national wildlife refuge for their winter home, a place not likely to undergo 'civilizing' alterations. Men of the United States Fish and Wildlife Service watched over the cranes, guarding and studying them. Crip and Jose-

Whooping Crane

phine became the first captive birds when they were rescued after having been injured. Otherwise they might have died in the wilderness.

The location of the summer nesting grounds in Canada remained a mystery for many years. American and Canadian wildlife experts searched 65,000 miles of northern Canada without seeing a whooping crane. Two were sighted in 1952 near the Great Slave Lake, and eight more were seen there the following year. The actual discovery of the nesting grounds was made in June 1954, by accident. A forest fire broke out in Wood Buffalo National Park, an 11-million-acre preserve four hundred miles south of the Arctic Circle. Canadian rangers mapping the blaze by helicopter unexpectedly caught sight of two adult whoopers and one young one. The following spring, a team from the Canadian Wildlife Service explored the park, which is bigger than Massachusetts, Connecticut, Rhode Island, and Delaware combined, and provides a home for many rare animals. (The largest wild herd of bison in the world lives there.) Near a small stream called the Sass River they found a rough nest of weeds and rushes – the first summer nest of a whooping crane seen since 1922.

The whoopers have now been thoroughly studied, both in their Canadian and Texan nesting grounds. Much is known about them that was unknown just a few years ago. They mate for life, and live in tight family groups; the males are aggressive and belligerent, the females placid and mainly concerned with raising the young. Each pair has one or two chicks at most in a season, and does not necessarily produce offspring every year. The young cranes are wobbly at first and are covered with fuzzy reddish-brown feathers, and the white feathers of maturity begin to appear after a few months, giving them a mottled calico appearance. By the time the new cranes are five months old, in the autumn, they are strong enough to make the 2,500-mile flight south. During the winter months their sleek white plumage completely replaces the reddish brown feathers, so that they become graceful smaller versions of their parents. When they are ready to return to Canada in April, it is hard to tell them from the older birds.

Each family picks out its own territory in the winter nesting grounds, occupying a four-hundred-acre tract. The entire whooper population dwells in a strip of ponds and salt flats a mile wide and fourteen miles long down the Gulf Coast. They rise at dawn and hunt crabs, fish, and molluscs in the ponds. A bird who trespasses on another bird's territory is met and driven off by the head of the family with loud whoops of rage. When spring draws near, the birds begin to do frantic little dances, leaping several feet off the ground with their legs stiff and their bills pointed skyward, and finally the whole flock takes to the sky, heading back to Canada to lay and hatch the year's eggs and raise the young.

The whooping crane is the tallest bird native to North America, and one of the most majestic anywhere in the world. Its extinction, which seemed inevitable a generation ago, has been postponed for a while through careful protection. With luck, it may survive a few decades longer. Since just one small flock remains, running a gauntlet of weapons twice a year, the risks of extinction are very high. An unexpected storm out of the Gulf of Mexico one autumn, a fire out of control in the Canadian woods some summer, and the species could easily be reduced past the point of survival.

The Javan Rhinoceros

One of the rarest large mammals of the world is the Javan rhinoceros, of which less than twenty-four remain. All types of rhinoceroses are scarce and threatened with extinction, but the Javan species is closest to making its exit.

The rhinoceros is a relic of a vanished era of bulky mammals. Some 30 million years ago rhinoceroses of all sizes and shapes were found throughout the world, some as small as sheep dogs, others giants like *Baluchitherium*,

Javan Rhinoceros

which stood eighteen feet tall. There were rhinos in North America until ten or fifteen thousand years ago. Europeans of the ice ages hunted woolly rhinoceroses in the cave era. Most of the big rhinos, though, became extinct long before man appeared on the scene. The rhinoceros was an animal on a downward trend a million years in the past.

Man the hunter had little interest in eating rhinos, but

man the healer found supposed medical uses for them. Chinese doctors came to use the powdered horns of rhinos as ingredients in drugs that were thought to cure epilepsy, stomach ailments, and dozens of other diseases. A cup made from rhinoceros horn allegedly rendered any poison harmless. As these superstitions took hold, the demand for rhinoceros horn became huge. Chinese pharmacists were willing to pay steep prices for the horns, since their patients would pay even steeper prices for the drugs made from them. All over Asia, rhinoceroses were mercilessly hunted. When sea trade began between Africa and China, the African rhinos became targets as well. One rhinoceros horn meant one dead rhino. The killing went on for centuries – and, since superstitions die hard, the killing is still going on. Though rhinos are protected by law in every land, poachers take the risk of arrest to shoot rhinos for their horns. The huge carcasses are left to rot, and the valuable horns find their way to the dark, antiquated druggists' shops of Hong Kong and Singapore, Shanghai and Peking.

Of the surviving species of rhinoceros, the most numerous is the black rhinoceros of Africa. This is the rhino commonly seen in zoos. It is a large two-horned animal with a dark brown or grey hide. Its temper is unpredictable and it can be a dangerous animal, charging men or motor cars at speeds that reach forty-five miles an hour. About thirteen thousand of these rhinoceroses live in eastern and central Africa.

The only other African species is the white rhinoceros, also called the square-lipped rhinoceros. This, too, is a two-horned rhino, light grey in colour and much bigger than the black rhinoceros. This blunt-nosed eater of grass and shrubbery stands six feet high at the shoulders, reaches lengths of fifteen feet, and weighs as much as $3\frac{1}{2}$ tons. It is a sociable beast usually found in groups of six or seven. About two hundred white rhinos are left in the wild, seventy of them in Uganda and most of the others in the Sudan. The front horn of a white rhino, which can be as long as three feet, fetches about £600 from a Chinese pharmacist, and this has led to considerable poaching on the remaining herds. African wildlife experts are trying to collect the surviving white rhinos and place them on protected reservations.

Black Rhinoceros

The rhinoceroses of Asia are of three main kinds. The Sumatran rhinoceros, the smallest living rhino, weighs about a ton and is three to four feet tall at the shoulders. It has two horns, and spends much of its time in mud wallows. Coarse black bristles sprout from its thick hide. These rhinos have been extensively hunted to supply the drug trade, and only about two hundred are thought to exist. They are found in Malaya, Borneo, Sumatra, and Burma.

Quite different is the Indian rhinoceros. It has only one horn and its skin is a thick, tough hide divided into great rigid slabs that look like armour plates. Though smaller than the African rhinos, it weighs nearly as much. This strange beast, which has the look of some prehistoric monster, is found only in north-east India. A population of about six hundred is known to exist.

The white, Sumatran, and Indian rhinoceroses, numbering about a thousand for the three species, are commonplace creatures compared with the Javan rhinoceros. This one-horned, armour-skinned beast is similar to the Indian rhino, but smaller in size. Its horn is also smaller, and the pattern of its skin folds is different, being divided into small scale-like discs, giving it a cracked look.

The first Javan rhinoceros was discovered in 1811, and it was recognized to be a distinct species nine years later. Though scarce, it was observed in the nineteenth century in Java, Sumatra, Malaya, Burma, Siam, Borneo, and other parts of south-east Asia. Like all rhinos, it had strictly vegetarian habits, browsing on leaves and twigs in swampy regions. As late as the 1870s it was still relatively abundant, since its small horn did not have much value to Oriental druggists.

The white colonial masters of the countries of southeast Asia fancied themselves as rhinoceros-hunters, though. Life was dull for these English, French, and Dutch administrators, and they made their stay in the sultry tropics more lively by organizing jungle safaris. The sluggish, harmless Javan rhinoceros was very little like the swift, violent black rhino of Africa that has provided so much excitement for hunters on that continent, but it was the best that this part of the world had to offer. Determined sportsmen slogged into the rhino swamps and shot the animals down as they wallowed in the mud.

It was customary for Europeans who had hunted in the tropics to publish memoirs of their adventures in slaughter. One such literary hunter admitted in print with some pride that he had killed up to 44 rhinos in a single day, letting about as many wounded ones escape. It took about thirty years of such exploits to exterminate the Javan rhinoceros throughout most of its range.

Only on Java and Sumatra did it still exist at the beginning of this century. The Javan rhino population was about fifty, and there were about a dozen on Sumatra. A white big-game hunter who lived in Sumatra in the 1920s made it a hobby to kill these rhinos, and personally accounted for seven of them in a few years' time. His friends dealt with the others.

In 1930 the Dutch authorities on Java ordered a halt to the carnage. The twenty remaining Javan rhinos were placed on the Udjung Kulon Nature Reserve in western Java, and further hunting was forbidden. Under police protection, the rhino herd slowly increased. Rhinos have long life spans – half a century or more – and like most long-lived animals produce relatively few offspring. However, at the outbreak of the Second World War there were about thirty rhinos in the preserve, a 50 per cent increase in a decade.

During the war, the Japanese drove out the Dutch administrators, and when the Japanese in turn were expelled, Java and the rest of Indonesia gained its independence. The new native rulers maintained the protected status of the Javan rhinoceros, but the early years of independence were chaotic and it was difficult to enforce the laws. Now that the Indian rhino was nearly extinct, the Javan rhino became valuable for its horn, and poachers broke into the reserve. Several of the rhinos were killed before order was restored.

Today no more than two dozen of the armoured one-horned rhinos still live in the sixty-five thousand swampy acres of the Javan sanctuary. By day they remain out of sight in the dense jungle vegetation, emerging at night to feed and bathe in the mud. Whether these rhinos still actually exist is open to some question, for Indonesia has been torn by political upheavals since October of 1965, and nature preserves are often left unguarded during revolutions and civil wars. Chinese merchants in Java are willing to buy rhino horns at a price of one half their weight in gold. Poachers may already have slain the last of these rhinoceroses.

What Can be Done?

Dozens of the world's large mammals are on the danger list, as well as many birds, reptiles, and fish. Year by year these imperilled species come closer to extinction. Many animals have vanished in the last several centuries. Good fortune has restored to us the cahow, the trumpeter swan, the nene, and a few other rare creatures. But we are not likely to get the others back. The great auk and the dodo are gone for ever. The oryx, the Javan rhinoceros, and the whooping crane may soon follow.

What can be done to save the animals now nearing extinction?

Man will not relinquish his hard-won domain. New roads will slash through fields and forests; houses and factories will rise in peaceful woodlands; waste products of all kinds will pour into streams and lakes and into the atmosphere. There are more than three thousand million human beings in the world today, and if present trends continue, there may be twice as many by the end of the century. That will leave little enough room for man himself, and none at all for wild animals.

The only way wildlife can survive on this planet is through the conscious effort of mankind. We who are crowding all other forms of life into extinction must take steps to save the creatures that remain, lest we find ourselves inhabiting a world in which we are alone.

Until the late nineteenth century almost nothing was done to rescue the vanishing animals. A few voices spoke out for conservation, but were not heard, Kings and dukes might collect rare animals for their private parks, but all too often these animals were killed by poachers or marauding soldiers, or simply turned into targets for the guns of bored aristocrats. That any government should attempt to conserve natural resources of any kind was unthinkable. In the United States, particularly, unlimited hunting, logging, and mining worked terrible destruction. In Australia, too, the unique animals of a virgin continent were exploited at great cost. The explosion of population into previously isolated island groups like the Mascarenes, Hawaii, and New Zealand brought death to many unprotected creatures.

Only when it began to seem that all wildlife would perish did private groups come forward to intervene. One of the earliest conservation organizations in the United States was the Audubon Society, founded in New York in 1886 and named after the great naturalist. This group grew until in 1905 it was nationally chartered as the National Association of Audubon Societies for the Protection of Wild Birds and Animals, simplified in 1940 to the National Audubon Society.

The Audubon Society and other pioneer conservationist groups worked hard to halt the slaughter of America's birds and mammals. Such birds as the egret, the heron, the spoonbill, the gull, and the tern were being hunted for their ornamental plumage; others were killed for their meat. The societies hired wardens to protect the nesting grounds of these birds, and urged state and federal governments to pass game laws. Several Audubon Society wardens were murdered by angry hunters early in this century, but their deaths only helped to focus public attention on the situation. President Theodore Roosevelt though an ardent big-game hunter, lent the authority of the White House to the campaign. He recognized that if unrestrained killing continued, no game would be left for sportsmen to hunt, and he had many wild areas of the country set aside as national parks, where hunting was totally forbidden.

In 1910 New York State passed the Audubon Plumage Bill, forbidding the sale of most wild-bird plumage in New York. That put a stop to much of the trade in that commodity in the entire country. Three years later, the federal government prohibited the importation of such plumes, which made it unprofitable to hunt them abroad. Other laws went on the books at the same time, such as the international seal treaty of 1911, and the sea-otter treaty of 1910.

Gradually the rarest of animals came under full protection, and the rest were placed under partial safeguards that enabled them to hold their own. National parks and national monuments came to include more than sixteen thousand square miles of the United States and its territories. A system of federal wildlife refuges grew, also, until today there are nearly three hundred of them, covering 28 million acres. Groups such as the Fauna Preservation Society, the Wildfowl Trust, and the International Committee for Bird Protection came into existence to perform the same task of arousing public opinion. In Poland, a League for Nature Protection was founded in 1927. France passed its first conservation laws in 1906, Denmark in 1917, Finland in 1924. Germany set aside 350,000 acres as reserves. Sweden established a dozen national parks. The Soviet Union designated forty areas, covering 3,700,000 acres, as wildlife sanctuaries. In Africa giant national parks covering thousands of square miles were created.

These were positive measures that did much to halt the pace of destruction. The numerous zoos that raised and bred rare animals contributed greatly also. 'Survival centres' in New York, London, and other cities concentrated on multiplying the existing captive herds of such scarce creatures as the white rhinoceros, Père David's deer, and the Arabian oryx.

Yet protective laws and national parks could not provide perfect safety for the world's threatened wildlife. Laws do not keep unscrupulous men from shooting at whooping cranes when no one is watching. Laws do not prevent starving peasants from breaking into wildlife sanctuaries to poach. Laws cannot stop rioting revolutionaries from killing rare animals. The sweeping political changes in Africa and Asia have seen many game preserves pass into the hands of native administrators who are unable or unwilling to provide proper security for the animals in their care. The losses to poachers in Africa have been particularly severe since 1960.

Even in the United States the protected animals are not totally safe. A government economy move in 1965 led to the proposed abolition or reduction in size of eleven wildlife refuges. For example, the elimination of a

49,000-acre sanctuary in South Carolina was suggested to save the government $37,000, about £13,000, a year. Such false economies have frequently led to the loss of protected areas. Building dams or highways in wildlife refuges has also caused harm to nature.

Where sanctuaries are under control of state or local governments, sudden shifts in policy may occur as the result of an election or after a change in official staff. One such instance occurred in 1964 when the state of Arizona astonished conservationists by announcing a legal hunting season for the Kaibab squirrel that lives north of the Grand Canyon. Since only a thousand Kaibab squirrels exist, hunting these few survivors hardly seemed desirable. Under great pressure from conservation groups all over the country, the Arizona game commission ultimately cancelled the squirrel hunt. But such episodes of thoughtlessness frequently occur, forcing the guardians of our wildlife to keep steady watch on changes in local regulations.

The most recent and most ambitious of the conservationist organizations is the World Wildlife Fund, founded in 1961. This international group is a tax-exempt charitable foundation that receives contributions from millionaires and school children alike, and puts the money to work rescuing the animals most urgently in need of help.

The World Wildlife Fund now serves as a general coordinating body, bringing together the different national conservation bodies in an organized crusade. Its projects, large and small, have done much to hold back the decline in wildlife population. The first public report of the Fund, called *The Launching of a New Ark*, was released in 1965. Among the many accomplishments it listed were these:

The purchase of twenty-five square miles of marshland in Spain, the last known habitat of the Spanish lynx, the Spanish imperial eagle, and the Spanish flamingo.

The acquisition of four oryxes for the Phoenix herd.

Paying the cost of shipping thirty nene from the Wildfowl Trust flock in England to the island of Maui, Hawaii.

Appropriation of £1,600 to build roads for wardens in the Meru District Game Reserve, Kenya.

A grant of £1,780 to establish a breeding colony of the scarce Hunter's antelope at the Tsavo East National Park, Kenya.

Provision of £4,450 to buy an aeroplane for the Kenya Game Department, permitting the wardens to control poaching.

A grant of £143 to build a fence around a nesting site of terns in England.

£160 to finance a study of the giant grebe of Guatemala, a large waterfowl down to two hundred individuals living on a single lake.

These and dozens of other projects are helping to rescue wildlife in many parts of the world. Unlike a government body, the World Wildlife Fund can move swiftly to deal with an emergency situation. Its offices throughout the world receive contributions to support this work. The British headquarters is at 7/8 Plum Tree Court, London, E.C.4.

We share our world with a wide variety of interesting and unusual animals. We have not been very good custodians of our fellow creatures, and some have been lost beyond recovery through greed or mere carelessness. It lies within our power to destroy all those that remain, for there is no animal so fierce, so savage, so swift, that it can escape man's weapons.

The Dodo, the Auk and the Oryx

It also lies within our power to preserve our wildlife heritage, to act as guardians of that heritage for those who follow after us. The list of recently extinct animals is a long one. Let it be said of the twentieth century that we kept that list from growing longer.

Further Reading and Index

For Further Reading

The following books are general works on natural history or conservation. They deal with many of the animals discussed in this book, and it is more practical to list them in one group than to include them in the chapter-by-chapter bibliography below:

HEUVELMANS, BERNARD: *On the Track of Unknown Animals* (Rupert Hart-Davis, London, 1958). Many animals.

PENNANT, THOMAS: *History of Quadrupeds* (B. White, London, 1781). Eighteenth-century account of the animal kingdom.

SILVERBERG, ROBERT: *Forgotten by Time* (Thomas Y. Crowell, New York, 1966). A survey of living fossils and a general introduction to the animal kingdom.

WENDT, HERBERT: *Out of Noah's Ark* (Weidenfeld & Nicolson, London, 1959). Sections on the sea cow, dodo, rhinoceros, great auk, and many other animals, well illustrated with early prints.

For material on individual themes, see the chapter lists below.

The Dodo, the Auk and the Oryx

Chapter 1: *The Idea of Extinction*

LUCRETIUS: *On the Nature of Things*. Among many translations, see the one by R. E. Latham (Penguin Books, Harmondsworth, 1951).

NEWELL, NORMAN D.: 'Crises in the History of Life', *Scientific American*, February 1963. A review of extinctions beginning with the trilobites.

SILVERBERG, ROBERT: *Man Before Adam* (Macrae Smith, Philadelphia, 1964). Considerable material on the theory of evolution.

TOLMACHOFF, I. P.: 'Extinction and Extermination', Smithsonian Institution Annual Report, 1929.

Chapter 2: *The Dodo*

FRIEDMANN, HERBERT: 'New Light on the Dodo and Its Illustrators', Smithsonian Institution Annual Report, 1955.

KEYNES, QUENTIN: 'Mauritius, Island of the Dodo', *National Geographic Magazine*, January 1956.

LEY, WILLY: 'Hunting Down the Dodo', *Galaxy*, October and November 1957.

OLIVER, CAPTAIN PASFIELD, editor: *The Travels of François Leguat* (Hakluyt Society, London, 1891).

TEMPLE, SIR RICHARD CARNAC, editor: *The Travels of Peter Mundy* (Hakluyt Society, London, 1914, 1919).

Chapter 3: *The Aurochs and the Bison*

CAESAR, JULIUS: *The Conquest of Gaul*. Among many translations, see the one by S. A. Handford (Penguin Books, Harmondsworth, 1951).

PLINY: *Natural History*. Translated by John Bostock and H. T. Riley (Henry G. Bohn, London, 1855).

See also Wendt.

Chapter 4: *Steller's Sea Cow*

GOLDER, F. A.: *Bering's Voyages* (American Geographical Society, New York, 1922). Logbooks and other primary data on the expeditions.

NORDENSKIÖLD, A. E.: *The Voyage of the Vega* (Macmillan & Company, London, 1881). One of the great books of exploration.

SUTTON, ANN and MYRON: 'The Adventures of Steller', *Natural History*, November 1956.

Chapter 5: *The Great Auk*

BROOKS, MAJOR ALLAN: 'Auks and Their Northland Neighbours', *National Geographical Magazine*, January 1936.
See also Wendt.

Chapter 6: *The Quagga*

WILLOUGHBY, DAVID P.: 'The Vanished Quagga', *Natural History*, February 1966.
See also Pennant.

Chapter 7: *The Moa and the Rukh*

DEEVEY, EDWARD S. JR.: 'The End of the Moas', *Scientific American*, February 1954.

LEY, WILLY: 'The Last of the Moas', *Galaxy*, September 1958.

YULE, SIR HENRY, editor: *The Book of Ser Marco Polo,* third edition, revised by Henri Cordier (John Murray, London, 1929). Background of the legend of the rukh.
See also Heuvelmans and Wendt.

Chapter 8: *The Giant Ground Sloth*

LEY, WILLY: 'Dead or Alive?', *Galaxy*, December 1959. *See also* Heuvelmans and Wendt.

Chapter 9: *The Passenger Pigeon and the Heath Hen*

MEE, CHARLES, L., JR.: 'Audubon in the Original', *American Heritage*, February 1966.

OGBURN, CHARLTON, JR.: 'The Passing of the Passenger Pigeon', *American Heritage*, June 1961. *See also Wendt*

Chapter 10: *Back from Oblivion*

Notornis
SMITH, R. V. FRANCIS: 'Finding an "Extinct" New Zealand Bird', *National Geographical Magazine*, March 1952.
See also Heuvelmans, Wendt.
Cahow
MURPHY, ROBERT and GRACE: 'The Cahow Still Lives', *Natural History*, April 1951.
Przewalski's Horse
See Heuvelmans, Wendt.

Chapter 11: *Saved at the Brink*

Père David's Deer
See Heuvelmans, Wendt.
Nene
RIPLEY, S. DILLON: 'Saving the Nene, World's Rarest Goose', *National Geographic Magazine*, November 1965.

Chapter 12: *On Their Way Out*

Oryx
See Heuvelmans, Wendt.

Whooping Crane
ALLEN, ROBERT PORTER: 'Whooping Cranes Fight for Survival', *National Geographic Magazine*, November 1959.

Javan Rhinoceros
VOS, ANTON DE, and HOOGERWERF, A.: 'Java's One-Horned Rhino', *Nature Magazine*, June–July 1950.

What Can Be Done?
BAKER, JOHN H.: 'Saving Man's Wildlife Heritage', *National Geographic Magazine*, November 1954.

JACKSON, HARTLEY H. T.: 'Conserving Endangered Wildlife Species', Smithsonian Institution Annual Report, 1945.

H.R.H. the Prince Philip, Duke of Edinburgh: 'Man's Wildlife Heritage Faces Extinction', *National Geographic Magazine*, November 1962.

SCOTT, PETER, editor: *The Launching of a New Ark*. First report of the World Wildlife Fund (Collins, London, 1965).

Index

Index

*There are now more than 600
Puffins to choose from, and some
of them are described on the
following pages.*

Pilgrims of the Wild
Grey Owl

Grey Owl was a successful guide and trapper in the Canadian backwoods. When he returned to his hunting grounds after the First World War he found that the get-rich-quick trappers had driven the wildlife northwards, and he resolved to follow them. The winter he adopted two orphaned kitten beavers changed his way of life.

Living with the beavers at such close quarters, and worrying that the wildlife was rapidly disappearing, Grey Owl gave up trapping altogether and instead began to work for the preservation of wildlife, and the beavers in particular. It is intriguing to think that nearly fifty years ago Grey Owl had the vision and foresight to realize what was happening, and the determination to do something about it.

Watership Down
Richard Adams

One dim, moonlit night a small band of rabbits leave the comfort and safety of their warren and set out on a long and dangerous journey. Not one of them knows where they are heading; neither Hazel, their courageous and unassuming leader, nor Bigwig, the brave and impetuous warrior, nor even Fiver, the prophet who provided them with the impetus to go with his vision of 'some terrible thing coming closer and closer' and a field 'covered with blood'.

This is a book about rabbits – *real* rabbits, who act throughout in accordance with real rabbit behaviour. It is a very special book – once you have read it you will understand what we mean. It won the Guardian Award and the Carnegie Medal in 1973.

Break for Freedom

Ewan Clarkson

Syla was a mink, and so dark brown she looked almost black.

The cage where she lived was identical with all the others, except for one thing – there was a loose staple in the floor of her sleeping box. And that was the way that Syla escaped from the fur farm to find a new life, free in a remote valley on the edge of Dartmoor, free to hunt and fish and play, and also to face the dangers of traps or sudden chills or fierce animals.

Ewan Clarkson is an expert naturalist and makes a fascinating story of Syla's year on the moor, her brief courtship with another escaped mink and her life with her cubs. At the same time he tells us about all the other inhabitants of Dartmoor, the birds and insects, snakes and rodents, till the moor seems as busy and complicated as the greatest human city.

For readers of eleven upwards.

Come Home, Brumby

Mary Elwyn Patchett

Fifteen-year-old Joey had for years dreamed of fencing in the brumby herd and breeding to improve the stock, so when Florian, the beautiful white stallion he had tamed, escaped to follow Brumby the wild stallion and his herd on their seasonal migration, he decided to follow the herd and find them somehow and drive them home single-handed.

The Custer Wolf

Roger Caras

One April five wolf cubs were born in a cave under a tree stump. One was white, and men would come to call him by a name that would live in history, for this was the beginning of the legend of the Custer Wolf.

This wolf inexplicably grew up different from any other. He was a beautiful but solitary animal and as he grew it became clear that he killed for the love of killing and terrorized a huge area round the town of Custer for six whole years.

Sometimes he killed thirty cattle in a week, more than he could possibly eat, and he took incredible chances, yet he escaped every trap that was set and every gun that was fired. Small wonder that the men believed the white wolf was charmed.

Tarka the Otter

Henry Williamson

This story of an otter is as true as long observations and keen insight could make it. It lets you live with Tarka and see at his level (much closer to the ground than our eye level) the wildlife of that stretch of Devon country which runs from Dartmoor to the sea, between the rivers Torridge and Taw. With a good map you can follow almost every step of the story.

To read Tarka for the first time is a tremendous experience whatever your age. It would be a pity to try it too young, but most people over ten will enjoy it.

If you have enjoyed this book and would like
to know about others which we publish, why
not join the Puffin Club? You will receive the
club magazine, *Puffin Post*, four times a year
and a smart badge and membership book.
You will also be able to enter all the
competitions. For details send a stamped
addressed envelope to:

The Puffin Club, Dept. A
Penguin Books Limited
Bath Road
Harmondsworth
Middlesex